The Somatic Therapy *Bible*

3 in 1

[3 in 1] The Ultimate Guide to Start Your Healing Journey to Overcome Past Trauma & Chronic Stress | With Daily Effective Techniques to Strengthen the Mind-Body Connection

By Sadie L. Miles

Table of Contents

Part I: Understanding Somatic Therapy | 10

Chapter 1: Introduction to Somatic Therapy | 11
What is Somatic Therapy? | **13**
The Good Old Definition | 13
History and Evolution | **14**
How the Ancient Cultures Viewed the Mind-Body Connection | 14
How Somatic Therapy Developed | 15
In Modern Times | 16
The Mind-Body Connection: Exploring Interconnectedness | **18**
The Academic Understanding | 19
Why Somatic Therapy Stands Out? | 20
Chapter Summary | **23**

Chapter 2: Exploring Trauma and Chronic Stress | 24
Understanding Trauma and Its Multifaceted Effects | **26**
Types of Trauma | 26
Trauma and the Brain | 27
Somatic Therapy and Trauma | 28
The Role of Resilience | 30
Chronic Stress: Its Subtle and Profound Impact on the Body | **31**
Stress | 31
Distress | 31
Eustress | 31
Chronic Stress | 32
Physical Impact of Chronic Stress on the Body | 32
Somatic Therapy and Chronic Stress | 34
Recognizing Symptoms and Signs: A Comprehensive Approach | **35**
Trauma: Signs and Symptoms | 35
Chronic Stress: Signs and Symptoms | 37
How to Move Forward | **39**

Chapter 3: Science Behind Somatic Healing | 41

Neurobiology of Trauma: Unraveling the Brain-Body Nexus 42
Brain-Body Nexus Illustrated 43
Key Features of the Brain-Body Nexus Summarized 44
Somatic Therapy's Influence on Neural Pathways 45
Understanding Neuroplasticity 45
How Somatic Therapy Affects Our Neurobiology 46
Long-Term Effects on Neurological Health 48
Exploring Interoception 48
Research and Evidence: The Validity of Somatic Approaches 49
Empirical Studies and Clinical Trials 50
Neuroscientific Research 50
Comparison with Other Therapies 50
Qualitative Research and Case Studies 50
Limitations of Somatic Therapy Research 51
Is Somatic Therapy Promising? 52
Chapter Summary 54

Chapter 4: Types of Somatic Therapy Modalities 55
Embodied Practices: Body-Centered Therapies 56
Types of Body-Centered Techniques 57
Sensorimotor Psychotherapy: Engaging Body and Mind 58
What Sensorimotor Failure Looks Like? 59
Sensorimotor Therapy at Play 60
Dance/Movement Therapy: Expressive Pathways to Healing 61
When Our Bodies Communicate 62
Chapter Summary 64

Chapter 5: Real-Life Experiments and Stories in Somatic Therapy 66
Case Studies: Experiences of Individuals in Somatic Therapy 67
What is a Case Study? 67
Types of Case Studies Commonly Associated with Somatic Therapy 68
A Car Accident Survivor's Recovery Through Somatic Therapy 69
Overcoming Childhood Abuse Through Somatic Therapy 71
Personal Testimonials: Stories of Triumph and Transformation 73
Difference between Personal Testimonial and Case Study 73
Testaments to the Efficacy of Somatic Therapy 74
Applying Somatic Techniques in Daily Life: A Practical Roadmap 75
Weeks 1-4: Initial Assessment and Building Trust 75
Weeks 5-8: Developing Body Awareness 75

Weeks 9-16: Processing and Releasing Emotions   76
Weeks 17-24: Integration and Empowerment   76
Months 6-12: Advanced Practices and Deepening Understanding 76
Months 12 and Beyond: Ongoing Growth and Maintenance   77

Part II: Starting Your Healing Journey   79

Chapter 6: Getting Started with Somatic Therapy   80
Finding the Right Therapist or Practitioner: Factors to Consider **81**
Hallmarks of a Somatic Therapist   81
Factors to Consider   82
Red Flags to Avoid   83
The Power of Reviews and Testimonials   84
Tackling Budget Concerns   85
Establishing a Support System: Nurturing a Healing Environment **86**
Creating a Support Network   87
Fostering a Nurturing Environment   88
Setting Healing Intentions: Charting the Course for Recovery **89**
For a Person with Trauma: 90
For a Person with Chronic Stress: 90
Chapter Summary   **92**
Key Takeaways   92

Chapter 7: Tools and Techniques for Healing   94
Breathwork: Harnessing the Power of Breath for Healing   **95**
Effects of the Body's Stress Response on Breathing   96
Breathwork Techniques Used for Somatic Therapy   97
Somatic Experiencing: Engaging the Body's Wisdom   **100**
"The Body's Wisdom"   100
How Somatic Experiencing was Discovered   101
Somatic Experiencing: The Process   102
Body Scan and Progressive Muscle Relaxation Techniques   **104**
Body Scan Technique: 104
Muscle Relaxation Techniques: 105
Chapter Summary   106

Chapter 8: Navigating Emotional Release   108
Understanding Emotional Triggers: Unraveling Emotional Patterns **109**
Emotions Vs. Thoughts   109

Emotional Triggers   110
Emotional Patterns   112
Link between Patterns and Triggers   113
Processing and Releasing Stored Emotions: Safe and Effective Practices 114
Emotional Processing   114
Somatic Methods Used for Processing and Releasing Emotions   116
Self-Compassion in Healing: Cultivating a Gentle Approach   118

Chapter 9: Integrating Mindfulness and Meditation   122
Mindfulness Practices: Enhancing Body Awareness   123
The Science behind Mindfulness   124
Body Awareness and Mindfulness   125
Enhancing Body Awareness Through Mindfulness Techniques   127
Meditation Techniques for Healing Trauma   128
Common Misconceptions About Meditation: 129
Meditation's Versatility   130
Healing Trauma through Meditation   131
Mindfulness-Based Stress Reduction (MBSR) Strategies   133
Program Routine   134
Chapter Summary   136

Part III: Strengthening the Mind-Body Connection   138

Chapter 10: Daily Practices for Wellness   139
Morning Rituals for Grounding and Centering   140
Common Challenges of Establishing Morning Rituals   142
Grounding and Centering in the Morning   143
Integrating Somatic Techniques into Daily Life   145
Daily Life Habits Explained   145
Somatic Techniques for Daily Life   145
Time Recommendations   148
Evening Routines for Relaxation and Reflection   149
Additional Habits   151
Showcasing a Daily Wellness Schedule   152
Chapter Summary   154

Chapter 11: Holistic Approaches to Somatic Healing   156
Nutrition and Its Impact on Mental Health: A Holistic Perspective   157
Nutrition and Mental Health   159

A Quick Nutritional Guide   160

Will Nutrition Help the Somatic Therapy Outcome?   162

Yoga and Somatic Integration: Aligning Mind, Body, and Spirit   163

Yoga and Trauma   164

Yoga and Somatic Integration   164

Where to Start   165

Expressive Arts Therapy: Tapping into Creative Healing   167

The Concept of Creative Healing   168

How Expressive Arts Complement Somatic Therapy   169

Chapter Summary   171

Chapter 12: Long-Term Strategies for Sustained Healing   172

Building Resilience: Strengthening Emotional Foundations   173

Understanding Emotional Foundations   174

Cultivating Resilience   176

Preventing Relapse: Strategies for Maintaining Progress   177

Relapse Prevention Strategies   178

Continuing the Journey Beyond Therapy: Lifelong Learning and Growth 180

Chapter 13: Community and Collective Healing   183

Group Therapy and its Therapeutic Benefits   184

Is Group Therapy Viable for Somatic Therapy?   185

Cultivating Supportive Communities: Peer Support Networks   186

The Role of Culture and Traditions in Healing   187

Conclusion: Embracing Your Healing Journey   192

Celebrating Progress and Growth: Acknowledging Milestones   193

Embracing Self-Compassion and Self-Care: The Core of Healing   194

Moving Forward on Your Healing Path: Embracing Lifelong Transformation 195

PART I

Understanding Somatic Therapy

Chapter 1

Introduction to Somatic Therapy

In the gentle embrace of dawn, as the first rays of sunlight spill over the horizon, there's a world awakening to new possibilities. Somewhere in that world, there's you, frustrated with the toll life has taken, trying to find answers to your inexplicable condition, standing at the threshold of a journey. Somehow, you stumbled upon this book. Well, this isn't just any journey—it's a voyage towards healing, understanding the intricate dance between mind and body, and embracing somatic therapy's transformative power.

Picture this: a tranquil garden, vibrant and full of life. In the center, a tree stands tall, its roots delving deep into the earth, its branches reaching toward the sky. Much like yourself, this tree has weathered storms and basked in sunlight, growing stronger with each passing day. It's a symbol of resilience, a testament to the power of growth and renewal. Navigating the comprehensive information in this book is akin to exploring this garden, uncovering hidden paths, and learning from the tree's wisdom.

Our narrative begins not with complex theories or abstract concepts but with anecdotes and stories—stories of people just like you who have walked through the shadows of past trauma and chronic stress. Intertwined with the latest research and insights into somatic therapy, these stories serve as beacons, guiding us through the sometimes-murky waters of healing.

In these pages, you'll discover the essence of somatic therapy, a therapeutic approach that emphasizes the interconnectedness of mind and body. It's a pathway to healing that recognizes that our bodies hold memories, emotions, and wisdom often overlooked in our fast-paced world. Through daily, effective techniques, we'll explore how to strengthen this mind-body connection, empowering you to become the architect of your recovery.

As you read further, we'll demystify the science behind somatic therapy, ensuring that it remains accessible, engaging, and, most importantly, relevant to your life. You'll find anecdotes that resonate, strategies that can be applied, and a sense of community in the shared experiences of others.

So, as you turn these pages, remember that you're not just engaging with a book—you're taking the first step on a profound journey. A journey of self-discovery, healing, and growth without relying on prescriptions or costly therapies. A journey where each chapter brings you closer to a deeper understanding of yourself and the incredible strength that resides within you.

So, let's begin.

What is Somatic Therapy?

THE GOOD OLD DEFINITION

The belief that stress and trauma manifest physically is a fundamental concept in many psychological disciplines and holistic health approaches. This belief is based on the understanding that the mind and body are deeply interconnected, and emotional experiences, particularly those related to stress and trauma, can have tangible physical effects.

"Soma" refers to the body, particularly as distinct from the mind or psyche. In various contexts, such as "somatic therapy," it emphasizes the body's role in psychological and emotional processes. Somatic therapy is a therapeutic approach that emphasizes the connection between the mind and body in the healing process. It operates on the principle that trauma, stress, and emotional experiences can manifest physically in the body, often as tension or pain. The core idea behind somatic therapy is that individuals can achieve greater psychological and emotional well-being by addressing these physical manifestations.

Key aspects of somatic therapy include:

1. **Body Awareness**: Clients are encouraged to become more aware of their bodily sensations and feelings. This heightened awareness helps recognize and understand the physical expressions of their emotions and stress.

2. **Mind-Body Connection:** Somatic therapy focuses on the interconnectedness of the mind and body, exploring how mental and emotional issues can affect physical health and vice versa.

3. **Movement and Breathwork:** Techniques such as gentle movement, stretching, and controlled breathing are often used to release physical tension, improve bodily alignment, and enhance overall well-being.

4. **Processing Trauma:** By focusing on the physical sensations associated with traumatic memories, somatic therapy aims to help individuals process and release the trauma stored in their bodies.

5. **Stress and Emotion Regulation:** Somatic therapy teaches techniques to regulate stress and manage emotions, which can be particularly beneficial for those dealing with anxiety, depression, or post-traumatic stress disorder (PTSD).

6. **Therapeutic Touch:** In some forms of somatic therapy, therapeutic touch or massage may help release physical tension and improve the body's alignment and balance.

Somatic therapy is used in various settings, including individual therapy, group therapy, and workshops. It's suitable for a wide range of issues, from chronic stress and anxiety to trauma and PTSD. The approach is holistic, often integrated with other therapeutic methods, and tailored to each person's individual needs.

History and Evolution

HOW ANCIENT CULTURES VIEWED THE MIND-BODY CONNECTION

Diving into the historical perspectives on the mind-body connection, we find that ancient cultures intuitively understood this interplay long before modern science provided evidence for it.

In ancient China, traditional Chinese medicine (TCM) principles encapsulated a deep understanding of the mind-body relationship. The concept of Qi, or vital energy, is central to TCM, which flows through the body's meridians. This energy flow was seen as crucial not only for physical health but for emotional and mental well-being, too. The Chinese developed practices like acupuncture and tai chi, not merely as physical exercises or treatments but as ways to maintain harmony between the body and the mind. Their approach was holistic, seeing emotional disturbances as disruptions in Qi that could lead to physical ailments and vice versa.

Similarly, ancient India's Ayurveda, one of the world's oldest holistic healing systems, reflects a profound recognition of the mind-body connection. Rooted in the belief that health and wellness depend on a delicate balance between the mind, body, and spirit, Ayurveda incorporates various treatments, including dietary changes, herbal remedies, yoga, and meditation. These practices aimed to align and balance one's physical state with one's mental and spiritual health, indicating a deep understanding that the state of the mind directly influences bodily health.

In ancient Greece, Hippocrates, often called the father of Western medicine, also emphasized the importance of considering the whole person - body, mind, spirit, and environment - in healing. His humoral theory suggested that health depended on the balance of four bodily fluids, with imbalances leading to disease. This theory implicitly acknowledged the impact of emotional and mental states on physical health.

These ancient practices highlight a common thread: an inherent wisdom about the interconnectedness of our emotional, mental, and physical states. Long before modern psychology and medical science began exploring these connections, ancient cultures across the globe were already practicing health care that embodied the mind-body principle, viewing optimal health as the harmonious balance of these elements.

HOW SOMATIC THERAPY DEVELOPED

The origins of somatic therapy as we know it in modern psychology can be traced back to the early 20th century, a period marked by significant advancements in psychology and a growing interest in the connection between the mind and body. To reiterate, this therapy is grounded in the understanding that trauma and stress can manifest physically in the body and that addressing these somatic (bodily) experiences can lead to healing.

One of the key figures in the development of somatic therapy was Wilhelm Reich, a student of Sigmund Freud. Reich, diverging from Freud's focus on the psychoanalytic approach, emphasized the role of physical processes in psychological health. In the 1930s and 1940s, he developed the concept of "muscular armor" – physical tension that he believed was linked to repressed emotions and trauma.

Parallel to Reich's work, other pioneers contributed to the somatic approach. For instance, Elsa Gindler, a German educator, focused on body awareness and self-regulation techniques. Her work influenced a generation of therapists who began to incorporate body awareness into their practices.

In the 1970s and 1980s, somatic therapy gained more prominence with the development of various body-oriented therapies. Known contributors during this time included:

1. **Alexander Lowen:** Developed Bioenergetic Analysis, a therapy combining psychoanalytic concepts with bodywork to release repressed emotions.

2. **Peter Levine:** Introduced Somatic Experiencing, a method focused on resolving trauma symptoms by releasing pent-up survival energy and restoring bodily sensations.

3. **Thomas Hanna:** Known for developing Hanna Somatic Education, which emphasizes internal physical perception and movement re-education.

These approaches shared a common belief in the importance of the body in processing emotional and psychological experiences. They recognized that trauma and stress are not just mental or emotional experiences but are often deeply embedded in the physical self.

In recent decades, somatic therapy has evolved, integrating insights from neuroscience, psychology, and holistic health. It emphasizes mindfulness, body awareness, movement, and therapeutic touch as key elements in healing. The increasing recognition of the mind-body connection in medical and psychological research has further validated and expanded the applications of somatic therapy.

IN MODERN TIMES

Today, somatic therapy is a diverse field, encompassing a range of techniques and approaches, all centered on the principle that the body holds the key to understanding and healing the mind. It has evolved significantly, adapting and integrating contemporary scientific understanding, particularly from neuroscience and psychology. This evolution has led to a more nuanced approach to the mind-body connection and the development of various specialized techniques and methodologies. Key aspects of this evolution include:

1. **Neuroscientific Integration:** Modern somatic therapy increasingly incorporates findings from neuroscience. Understanding how trauma and stress affect the nervous system and brain has led to more effective therapeutic techniques that address these physiological changes.

2. **Trauma-Informed Approaches:** There's a greater focus on trauma-informed care, recognizing that trauma can have a profound and lasting impact on both the mind and body. Techniques in somatic therapy now often include elements specifically designed to address and heal trauma.

3. **Digital and Remote Therapies:** With the advent of digital communication, somatic therapy has expanded to include online and remote sessions, making it more accessible. Therapists use video calls and digital platforms to guide clients through exercises and provide support.

4. **Integration with Other Therapies:** Somatic therapy is increasingly combined with other therapeutic approaches, such as cognitive-behavioral therapy (CBT), mindfulness-based stress reduction (MBSR), and psychoanalysis, to provide a more comprehensive treatment.

5. **Diversity in Techniques:** The field has diversified to include a variety of techniques such as somatic experiencing, Hakomi, body-mind centering, and others, each with its unique approach to addressing the somatic aspects of mental health.

6. **Research and Evidence-Based Practice:** A growing body of research supports somatic therapy's efficacy. This research has helped in refining techniques and approaches, ensuring they are evidence-based and effective.

7. Holistic and Preventative Health: Modern somatic therapy often plays a role in holistic and preventative health care, focusing on treating symptoms, promoting overall wellness, and preventing future issues.

8. Cultural Sensitivity: Modern practices are increasingly acknowledging and incorporating cultural, social, and individual diversity, recognizing that different groups and individuals might experience and embody trauma and stress in varied ways.

9. Self-Care and Empowerment: There's a greater emphasis on teaching people self-care practices and empowering them to take an active role in their healing process, fostering long-term resilience and well-being.

In summary, modern somatic therapy is a dynamic and evolving field, increasingly informed by scientific research, adapting to new technologies, and expanding its techniques and approaches to cater to a diverse range of needs.

The Mind-Body Connection: Exploring Interconnectedness

Imagine Sarah, a graphic designer in her mid-30s. She's been working on a high-pressure project for weeks. In the starting stages, things were going well, but lately, she's been feeling this nagging tension in her neck and shoulders. No amount of stretching seems to help. It's like her body is holding onto the stress of her work.

Here's where the mind-body connection comes into play. Our bodies and minds are like best friends who share everything, including stress and worries. When Sarah's brain is on overdrive with deadlines and client demands, it sends signals to her body. Her muscles tense up as if bracing for impact – a physical manifestation of her mental load.

But it's not just a one-way street. Let's say Sarah decides to try a yoga class. She's focusing on her breath, moving through poses, and suddenly, she feels a bit lighter. That's because moving her body and focusing on her breathing sends a message back to her brain saying, "Hey, it's okay. We can relax." This physical activity helps lower her stress hormones, easing her mind.

And it goes even deeper. Ever heard of the placebo effect? It's like when you take a sugar pill thinking it's medicine, and somehow, you start feeling better. That's the mind convincing the body, "We've got medicine, it's going take care of the immune system, let's ramp up the healing cause we're going to get better," and the body listens!

But let's remember, it's a two-way street. If Sarah, for example, injures her ankle, it's not just her walking that's affected. She might start feeling down or frustrated because she can't be as active as she likes, showing how our physical state can influence our mood and mental health.

Many of us can relate to Sarah. The mind-body connection is all about this intricate dance between our thoughts, emotions, and physical sensations. It's a relationship where each partner influences the other, often in surprising ways. Understanding and nurturing this connection can be powerful in managing stress, healing, and overall well-being.

THE ACADEMIC UNDERSTANDING

That was the simple explanation, but let's go deeper with some technicalities. The mind-body connection is the profound and complex interplay between our mental, emotional, and physical states. It is a foundational concept in many holistic health approaches and is increasingly recognized in mainstream medicine. This connection implies that our thoughts, feelings, beliefs, and attitudes can positively or negatively affect our biological functioning, while what happens in our bodies can impact our mental health.

Several components constitute this complex connection. Let's take a look at some of them.

NEUROLOGICAL PATHWAYS

The brain communicates with the rest of the body via the nervous system. This communication system allows emotional and cognitive processes to influence physiological responses. For instance, when we perceive a threat, the brain triggers a stress response, releasing hormones like cortisol and adrenaline, which prepare the body to act.

PSYCHOSOMATIC RESPONSES

This term refers to physical symptoms that are caused or exacerbated by mental factors, such as stress, anxiety, and depression. Common examples include stress-induced headaches, stomach ulcers related to anxiety, or the exacerbation of skin conditions like eczema due to emotional stressors.

IMPACT OF STRESS

Chronic stress can lead to a range of physical health problems, including heart disease, high blood pressure, weakened immune function, and chronic pain. The body's stress response, meant to be short-term and protective, can become harmful when activated over a long period.

EMOTIONAL REGULATION AND PHYSICAL HEALTH

How we manage and express emotions can directly and indirectly affect our physical health. Poor emotional regulation can lead to unhealthy coping mechanisms (like smoking or overeating) that have detrimental physical effects.

MINDFULNESS AND BODY AWARENESS

Practices that enhance mindfulness and body awareness, such as meditation, yoga, and tai chi, can improve physical health. These practices reduce stress, lower blood pressure, improve heart health, and enhance immune function.

PSYCHONEUROIMMUNOLOGY

This field studies the link between the mind (psycho-), the brain and nervous system (neuro-), and the immune system (immunology). Research in this area has shown how mental states can affect the immune system, influencing our susceptibility to and recovery from illnesses.

PLACEBO EFFECT

This phenomenon, where people experience real changes in their health after receiving a treatment with no therapeutic effect, demonstrates the power of expectation and belief in physical health.

BI-DIRECTIONAL INFLUENCE

The mind-body connection is bi-directional. Physical illnesses and discomfort can impact mental health, leading to conditions like depression and anxiety, while good physical health can improve mental well-being.

Understanding and harnessing the mind-body connection is essential in somatic therapy and other holistic health practices. It emphasizes the importance of treating the whole person, acknowledging that improving mental health can lead to better physical health and vice versa.

WHY SOMATIC THERAPY STANDS OUT

There are so many therapeutic methods out there that it's natural to ask, "Why dabble in somatic therapy?" Understand that each approach is designed for a specific purpose, and the best recovery path is to diagnose your particular situation with the help of a counselor and tailor a combination of treatments. Let's stroll through the diverse world of psychological therapies and see where somatic therapy fits in and why it's unique.

1. **Cognitive Behavioral Therapy (CBT):** CBT is like the coach of therapies. It focuses on identifying and changing negative thought patterns and behaviors. It's practical, structured, and often short-term. CBT is like giving your mind a set of tools to fix faulty thinking patterns.

2. **Psychoanalysis and Psychodynamic Therapy:** These are the old souls of therapy. They delve deep into your past, especially childhood, to uncover the roots of your issues. It's like a detective exploring the hidden corners of your psyche to understand how your past shapes your present.

3. **Humanistic Therapy:** This approach is the empathetic friend. It emphasizes personal growth and self-fulfillment, focusing on your unique individual experience. It's about understanding and accepting yourself, creating a space where you feel heard and valued.

4. **Dialectical Behavior Therapy (DBT):** Think of DBT as the balancer. It's great for those who experience intense emotions. It combines CBT techniques with mindfulness, helping you balance accepting yourself while striving to change.

5. **Family and Systemic Therapy:** This one's the family mediator. It views problems within the context of the family or relationship system. It's like untangling a complicated web of interactions to find healthier ways for everyone to relate to each other.

Now, enter somatic therapy. Imagine it as the wise sage who reminds you that your body has a story to tell. Unlike therapies that focus mainly on thoughts or emotions, Somatic Therapy focuses on bodily experiences and physical sensations. It's grounded in the idea that our bodies hold onto emotions and traumas, often manifesting as physical symptoms or sensations.

What makes somatic therapy stand out is its focus on this mind-body connection. It's like conversing with your body, listening to its wisdom, and using that understanding to heal. Techniques might include breathwork, movement, or even therapeutic touch. It's especially powerful for people who have experienced trauma, as it helps to release the physical "memory" stored in the body.

So, while each therapy has unique approaches and strengths, somatic therapy stands out for its holistic integration of the physical body in the healing process. It's not just talking about feelings; it's about feeling them in a literal sense and using that to foster deep, lasting change.

Chapter Summary

In conclusion, the journey through the history and principles of somatic therapy reveals a timeless understanding of the mind-body connection. From the holistic practices of ancient civilizations like China's TCM and India's Ayurveda to the more contemporary somatic therapy approaches, this connection has been recognized as vital for overall health and well-being. These traditions and modern practices underscore a universal truth: our physical and emotional states are deeply intertwined, each profoundly influencing the other. This knowledge enriches our understanding of somatic therapy and offers valuable insights into how we can approach healing and wellness in a more integrated, holistic way.

In the next chapter, we'll delve into the world of trauma and chronic stress, unraveling how they affect us and why understanding them is crucial for healing and growth.

My Note

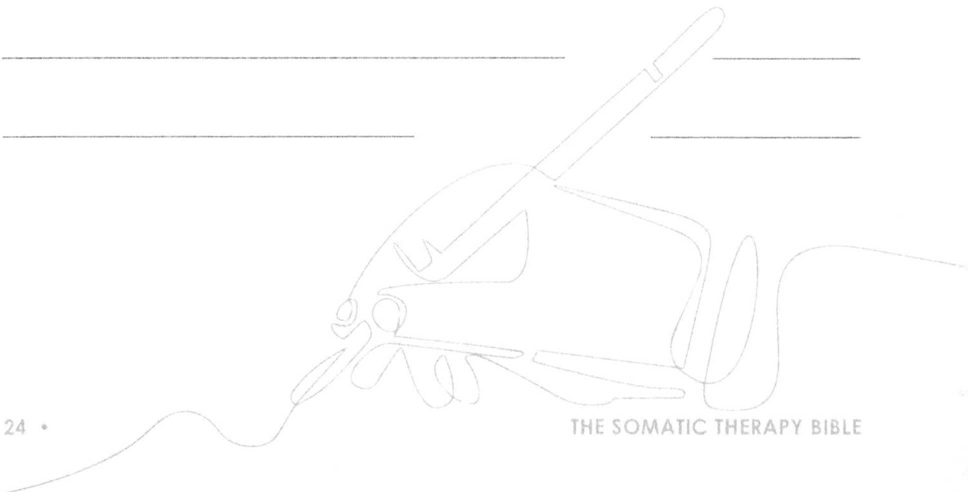

_____

_____

_____

_____

_____

_____

_____

_____

_____

_____

_____

_____

_____

_____

_____

_____

Chapter 2

Exploring Trauma and Chronic Stress

Now, we turn our focus to two pervasive and impactful aspects of human experience: trauma and chronic stress. Here, we aim to illuminate these often-misunderstood subjects and explore their profound effects on our lives.

Trauma, a response to deeply distressing or disturbing events, can shake the very foundation of our sense of safety and well-being. You have to think beyond the events themselves; the imprint of those experiences internalizes in your subconscious memory. Like an echo in a vast canyon, the impact of trauma can reverberate through our lives, manifesting in ways we might not immediately recognize.

Chronic stress, on the other hand, is the response to emotional pressure suffered for a prolonged period over which an individual perceives they have little or no control. It's more than the stress of a bad day or a hectic week; it's a constant burden that can lead to serious health issues, both mental and physical.

In this chapter, we'll understand the nature of trauma and chronic stress. We'll explore their symptoms, how they affect our minds and bodies, and most importantly, how they can be addressed and transformed. As we move through this chapter, keep in mind that recognizing and addressing trauma and chronic stress is a significant step towards healing, and a significant pathway in that recovery is somatic therapy.

Understanding Trauma and Its Multifaceted Effects

Trauma is a complex and multifaceted concept, often misunderstood or oversimplified. At its core, trauma is an emotional and psychological response to an event or series of events that are deeply distressing or disturbing to a person's psyche. It's important to recognize that trauma is highly subjective; what may be traumatic for one person might not be for another. The impact of trauma depends on various factors, including individual history, resilience, and the presence of supportive environments.

TYPES OF TRAUMA

1. Acute Trauma This results from a single distressing event, such as an accident, natural disaster, or violent attack.

Example: Imagine someone who witnesses a severe car accident. This singular, shocking event can result in acute trauma. In the aftermath, the individual might experience intense fear, anxiety, or distress when recalling the incident or even when hearing the sound of a car horn or seeing a similar road scene. This trauma is linked specifically to that one event.

2. Chronic Trauma This is repeated and prolonged exposure to highly stressful events, like domestic violence, abuse, or long-term illness.

Example: Consider a child growing up in a household with ongoing domestic violence. The child is exposed to repeated traumatic events over a prolonged period. This chronic exposure can lead to long-term emotional and psychological difficulties, such as trust issues, chronic anxiety, or a persistent sense of danger, as the trauma becomes ingrained in their day-to-day life.

3. Complex Trauma This involves exposure to multiple traumatic events, often of an invasive and interpersonal nature, leading to more severe impacts.

Example: A soldier deployed multiple times to war zones might experience complex trauma. This could stem from various sources, such as witnessing the death of comrades, engaging in combat, and the constant stress of living in a dangerous environment. The soldier may return with complex emotional and psychological issues, including PTSD, stemming from layered and interwoven traumatic experiences.

TRAUMA AND THE BRAIN

Trauma's impact on the brain is both profound and intricate, significantly affecting how we process, respond to, and recover from traumatic experiences. When a person experiences trauma, their brain undergoes several changes, particularly in regions responsible for emotion regulation, memory processing, and threat detection.

The **amygdala**, a key player in the brain's response to trauma, acts as an alarm system. It's responsible for detecting danger and triggering the body's fight-or-flight response. In the aftermath of trauma, the amygdala can become hyperactive. This heightened state leads to an increased stress response, making the individual more reactive to perceived threats. They may experience heightened anxiety, fear, or panic in situations that remind them of the trauma, even if these situations are not threatening.

Meanwhile, the **hippocampus,** which plays a crucial role in forming and retrieving memories, can be affected by trauma. Studies have shown that prolonged exposure to stress hormones like cortisol can impair the functioning of the hippocampus. This impairment can lead to difficulties forming new memories and processing the traumatic event. As a result, traumatic memories may not be properly integrated into the person's narrative memory, leading to flashbacks and intrusive thoughts where the trauma feels as though it's happening in the present.

The **prefrontal cortex,** responsible for higher-order functions like reasoning, impulse control, and decision-making, can also be impacted. After trauma, this region may become less effective in regulating emotions and responses. This can result in difficulties managing emotions, impulsivity, and challenges in making reasoned decisions, particularly in stressful situations.

These changes in the brain can contribute to the development of trauma-related disorders like post-traumatic stress disorder (PTSD). In PTSD, the brain remains in a heightened state of alertness, constantly on the lookout for danger. This can lead to symptoms like flashbacks, where the traumatic event is relived, nightmares, severe anxiety, and avoidance of anything that might recall the trauma.

Additionally, trauma can impact the brain's reward system, which can make individuals more susceptible to substance abuse as they might use drugs or alcohol to self-medicate and cope with their distress.

Understanding how trauma affects the brain is crucial, as it informs therapeutic approaches and strategies. Treatments like somatic therapy combined with other modalities can help retrain the brain's response to trauma, aiding in recovery and helping individuals regain a sense of safety and control. This brings us to our next point.

SOMATIC THERAPY AND TRAUMA

Somatic therapy offers a unique approach to dealing with trauma by focusing on the body's role in storing and processing traumatic experiences. This therapy is grounded in the understanding that trauma is not only a psychological phenomenon (in the mind) but also a somatic one (physically sensed in the body). Here's how somatic therapy can be particularly effective in treating trauma:

1. **Reconnecting with the Body:** Trauma can often lead to a disconnection from the body, a state known as dissociation, where individuals may feel numb or detached from their physical selves. Somatic therapy helps by encouraging a reconnection to the body through awareness of bodily sensations and experiences. This process can help individuals become more grounded and present.

2. **Releasing Trauma Stored in the Body:** Somatic therapy operates on the principle that the body holds onto traumatic experiences, often manifesting as chronic tension or pain. Through techniques like movement, breathwork, and sometimes therapeutic touch, somatic therapy aims to release this stored trauma. By addressing the physical manifestations of trauma, individuals can begin to process and heal from their experiences.

3. **Regulating the Nervous System:** Trauma can leave the nervous system in heightened danger arousal. Somatic therapy employs various exercises to help regulate the nervous system. Techniques such as deep breathing, mindfulness, and physical grounding exercises can shift the body from hyperarousal (associated with the fight-or-flight response) to a state of relaxation and balance.

4. **Empowering the Individual:** Somatic therapy often involves teaching individuals techniques they can practice independently. This empowerment is crucial to trauma recovery, as it helps individuals feel more in control of their bodies and emotions.

5. **Integrating Traumatic Memories:** By combining body-focused techniques with psychotherapy, somatic therapy can help in the integration of traumatic memories. This integration involves processing the trauma so that it becomes a part of the individual's story without continually retriggering the trauma response.

6. **Mind-Body Reconciliation:** Somatic therapy aids in reconciling the mind and body, helping individuals understand and appreciate how their bodies respond to trauma. This reconciliation can lead to a deeper sense of self-compassion and understanding.

In essence, somatic therapy addresses the physiological aspects of trauma, complementing traditional psychotherapy approaches that focus on the cognitive and emotional elements. This holistic approach can be particularly effective for individuals who have found limited relief in more traditional, talk-based therapies, offering a pathway to healing that engages the entire self – body and mind.

THE ROLE OF RESILIENCE

Resilience is significant in individual circumstances of trauma because it shapes how a person navigates and ultimately recovers from their traumatic experience. On a personal level, resilience involves the ability to withstand emotional upheaval, adapt to the stressors or changes brought about by trauma, and rebuild oneself in the aftermath. It's about how an individual copes with and processes traumatic events, utilizing internal and external resources. This could mean relying on inner strengths like a positive outlook or drawing support from relationships and community.

For example, one person might find strength in their ability to remain hopeful, while another might lean on a close-knit support network. Resilience doesn't negate the pain or difficulty of trauma. Still, it enables individuals to face their challenges, learn from them, and emerge with a deeper understanding of themselves and perhaps even a renewed sense of purpose. In this way, resilience is deeply personal and varies widely; it's shaped by an individual's unique experiences, personality, environment, and coping mechanisms.

Essentially, while it's true that trauma centers around specific events that have occurred in a person's past, healing from those traumatic experiences requires addressing the scars they leave behind. Understanding trauma – its causes, effects, and pathways to recovery – is essential for anyone looking to heal from their past and build a stronger, more resilient future.

Chronic Stress: Its Subtle and Profound Impact on the Body

Now we come to trauma's twin brother, often interchanged (wrongfully) and misidentified, chronic stress. Before we do that, let's create some important distinctions.

Stress is a broad term that encompasses various types of experiences and responses. The distinctions between stress, distress, eustress, and chronic stress are crucial for recognizing how these different forms of stress affect us and how we can manage them.

STRESS

At its core, stress is the body's response to any demand or challenge. Both positive and negative experiences can trigger it. When faced with a stressor (the cause or object of stress), the body responds with physical, mental, or emotional changes to adapt to that stressor. This response includes the release of hormones like adrenaline and cortisol, preparing the body to either confront or flee from the challenge (the fight-or-flight response).

DISTRESS

Distress refers to negative stress. This is the type of stress most people are familiar with. It occurs when the demands placed on an individual exceed their perceived ability to cope with the situation. Distress can be triggered by job loss, relationship problems, or financial difficulties. It's often associated with feelings of anxiety, sadness, or worry and can lead to physical symptoms like headaches, high blood pressure, and sleep disturbances.

EUSTRESS

Eustress, on the other hand, is positive stress. It's the kind of stress that feels exciting and motivating. Eustress is what you experience when taking on a challenging but enjoyable project, participating in a competitive sport, or planning a wedding. It's typically short-term and enhances your performance or enjoyment of a situation. Eustress can provide a sense of fulfillment or other positive feelings.

CHRONIC STRESS

Chronic stress is the response to emotional pressure suffered for a prolonged period over which an individual perceives they have little or no control. It occurs when a person faces continuous stressors without relief or relaxation between challenges, leading the body to constantly activate. This type of stress can have significant health implications, contributing to a range of issues from mental health conditions like anxiety and depression to physical problems like heart disease and a weakened immune system.

Understanding these different types of stress is important for effective stress management. While eustress can be beneficial and motivating, distress and chronic stress require management and coping strategies to prevent long-term harm to our mental and physical well-being.

PHYSICAL IMPACT OF CHRONIC STRESS ON THE BODY

Chronic stress exerts a significant physical impact on the body, affecting various systems and functions. When the body is subjected to prolonged periods of stress, the continuous activation of the stress response can lead to a range of health issues:

1. **Cardiovascular System:** Chronic stress increases heart rate and blood pressure, putting more strain on the heart. Over time, this can contribute to a higher risk of hypertension, heart attacks, or strokes. The ongoing release of stress hormones can raise cholesterol levels and promote artery-clogging.

2. **Immune System:** Initially, stress can boost the immune system. However, chronic stress weakens it, making the body less effective

at fighting off illnesses. This can lead to increased susceptibility to infections and slow the healing process.

3. **Digestive System:** Stress can affect the entire digestive system. It can cause issues like stomachaches, heartburn, acid reflux, and can exacerbate conditions like irritable bowel syndrome (IBS) and ulcers. Stress can also impact the absorption of nutrients and alter gut bacteria, contributing to gastrointestinal discomfort.

4. **Musculoskeletal System:** Chronic stress often leads to muscle tension, which can cause headaches, migraines, and chronic pain conditions such as tension-type headaches or myofascial pain syndrome. Over time, this constant muscle tension can contribute to musculoskeletal disorders.

5. **Endocrine System:** Stress stimulates the adrenal glands to produce cortisol and adrenaline, hormones that trigger the body's stress response. Over time, high levels of cortisol can disrupt the functioning of other hormones, contributing to issues like weight gain, osteoporosis, and even problems with menstrual cycles and reproductive health.

6. **Nervous System:** Chronic stress can impact brain function, including memory and concentration. It can alter brain chemistry, which may contribute to anxiety, depression, and other mental health disorders. Stress can also affect sleep patterns, leading to insomnia and reducing sleep quality.

7. **Metabolic Effects:** Chronic stress can affect metabolism. Elevated cortisol levels can lead to weight gain, as cortisol can increase appetite and encourage the body to store fat, particularly in the abdominal area.

In summary, chronic stress can take a toll on nearly every system in the body. By acquainting yourself with these impacts, you can manage stress and adopt lifestyle changes and coping strategies to mitigate these harmful effects, which is what we intend to do with somatic therapy.

SOMATIC THERAPY AND CHRONIC STRESS

Somatic therapy offers a unique approach to managing chronic stress by emphasizing the physical manifestations of stress and teaching individuals to actively engage with their bodily responses. This form of therapy operates on the understanding that chronic stress is not only a mental or emotional burden but also one that is deeply ingrained in the body. Through somatic therapy, individuals learn to become acutely aware of their bodily sensations - the tension in their muscles, the pattern of their breathing, and even their posture. This heightened body awareness is crucial, allowing individuals to recognize and respond to the first signs of stress.

A key aspect of somatic therapy is its focus on releasing physical tension and calming the body's stress response. Techniques such as deep breathing, guided movements, and mindful meditation are employed to soothe the nervous system, transitioning the body from a state of alert and arousal to one of relaxation and balance. This alleviates immediate stress symptoms and contributes to a longer-term resilience against stress.

Moreover, somatic therapy enhances the mind-body connection. It helps individuals understand how their thoughts and emotions are mirrored in their physical state. For someone dealing with chronic stress, this insight is invaluable. It shifts the perspective from feeling overwhelmed by stress to understanding and managing it through the body.

By teaching practical, body-based techniques, somatic therapy empowers individuals. They gain tools they can use daily, not just within the therapy session. This sense of empowerment is essential for individuals dealing with chronic stress, as it provides them with a sense of control and autonomy over their responses to stressors.

Essentially, somatic therapy addresses chronic stress from a holistic standpoint. It acknowledges the intertwined nature of the mind and body. It provides a pathway to manage stress rooted in physical experience and awareness, leading to more effective and sustainable stress management.

Recognizing Symptoms and Signs: A Comprehensive Approach

TRAUMA: SIGNS AND SYMPTOMS

Trauma can manifest through a wide range of signs and symptoms, affecting individuals on emotional, physical, and behavioral levels. These symptoms can vary greatly depending on the individual, the nature of the traumatic event, and other personal factors. Here's a detailed look at the various signs and symptoms of trauma:

EMOTIONAL SYMPTOMS

1. **Shock, Denial, or Disbelief:** Initially, individuals might feel numb or have difficulty accepting what happened.

2. **Confusion and Difficulty Concentrating:** Trauma can disrupt cognitive functions, focusing or thinking difficult.

3. **Anger, Irritability, Mood Swings:** People may experience intense and unpredictable emotions.

4. **Anxiety and Fear:** There's often a pervasive sense of anxiety or fear, particularly about a recurrence of a traumatic event.

5. **Guilt, Shame, Self-Blame:** Survivors might blame themselves or feel guilty about what occurred or how they responded.

6. **Withdrawing from Others:** Individuals may pull away from social interactions and feel detached.

7. **Feelings of Sadness or Hopelessness:** Prolonged feelings of sadness can occur, sometimes leading to depression.

8. **Feeling Numb or Disconnected:** Emotional numbing is a common way of coping with the intense and overwhelming emotions of trauma.

PHYSICAL SYMPTOMS

1. **Insomnia or Nightmares:** Trouble sleeping and distressing dreams are common.

2. **Being Startled Easily:** A heightened startle response is typical after trauma.

3. **Racing Heartbeat and Agitation:** These are signs of heightened arousal and anxiety.

4. **Aches and Pains:** Unexplained physical symptoms can occur like headaches, muscle pains, or stomach aches.

5. **Fatigue:** Feeling tired all the time is common, as trauma can be emotionally and physically exhausting.

6. **Edginess and Agitation:** Individuals may feel constantly on edge or nervous.

7. **Difficulty Concentrating:** Trauma can impact cognitive functions, making it hard to concentrate or make decisions.

BEHAVIORAL SYMPTOMS

1. **Avoidance of Reminders of Trauma:** This includes avoiding places, people, or activities that remind them of the event.

2. **Changes in Eating and Sleeping Habits:** This can include eating too much or too little or sleeping too much or too little.

3. **Increased Use of Alcohol or Drugs:** Some may use substances to try to numb their emotions.

4. **Social Withdrawal:** Pulling away from friends and family and losing interest in activities previously enjoyed.

5. **Self-Destructive Behavior:** This might include reckless driving, unprotected sex, or substance abuse.

1. **Post-Traumatic Stress Disorder (PTSD):** This includes symptoms like flashbacks, nightmares, severe anxiety, and uncontrollable thoughts about the traumatic event.

2. **Acute Stress Disorder:** Similar to PTSD, but the symptoms are temporary, usually lasting a few days to a month after the event.

3. **Depression:** Persistent feelings of sadness, hopelessness, and loss of interest in activities.

4. **Anxiety Disorders:** Generalized anxiety, panic attacks, or specific phobias.

Disclaimer: Experiencing trauma can affect people in different ways, and not everyone will have all these symptoms. The intensity and duration of symptoms can also vary.

CHRONIC STRESS: SIGNS AND SYMPTOMS

Chronic stress, a prolonged and constant feeling of stress, can manifest in various ways, much like trauma, impacting an individual's physical health, emotional well-being, cognitive abilities, and behavior. Here are detailed insights into the signs and symptoms of chronic stress:

PHYSICAL SYMPTOMS

1. **Headaches and Migraines**: Frequently occurring headaches can signify chronic stress.

2. **Muscle Tension and Pain:** Continuous stress often leads to muscle tension, especially in the neck, shoulders, and back, resulting in pain or discomfort.

3. **Fatigue:** Despite adequate sleep, individuals might feel persistently tired, a sign of the body's overexertion in managing stress.

4. **Digestive Issues:** Stress can affect the gastrointestinal system, leading

to symptoms like heartburn, acid reflux, constipation, or diarrhea.

5. **Cardiovascular Problems:** Increased heart rate, high blood pressure, and a heightened risk of heart disease are associated with chronic stress.

6. **Immune System Suppression:** Ongoing stress can weaken the immune system, leading to frequent colds, infections, and a slower healing process.

7. **Changes in Libido:** Chronic stress can affect sexual desire and performance.

EMOTIONAL AND PSYCHOLOGICAL SYMPTOMS

1. **Anxiety and Worry:** Constant worry about various aspects of life, often leading to anxiety disorders.

2. **Depression:** Long-term stress can contribute to feelings of hopelessness and sadness, potentially leading to depression.

3. **Irritability and Mood Swings:** Small issues may provoke irritation or anger more easily than usual.

4. **Feeling Overwhelmed:** A sense of being unable to cope with everyday tasks and responsibilities.

5. **Lack of Motivation or Focus:** Difficulty concentrating and a lack of interest in activities once enjoyed.

COGNITIVE SYMPTOMS

1. **Memory Problems:** Difficulty in remembering, concentrating, and making decisions.

2. **Constant Worrying:** An inability to stop worrying about various issues, including those that are not immediately pressing.

3. **Indecisiveness:** Difficulty in making decisions, even about simple matters.

BEHAVIORAL SYMPTOMS

1. **Changes in Appetite:** Either a loss of appetite or overeating can be a response to chronic stress.

2. **Sleep Disturbances:** Insomnia or sleeping too much, difficulty falling or staying asleep, and restless sleep.

3. **Increased Use of Alcohol, Tobacco, or Drugs:** Using substances to relax, escape, or numb feelings.

4. **Social Withdrawal:** Pulling away from social interactions and activities.

5. **Neglecting Responsibilities:** Difficulty in keeping up with personal or professional responsibilities.

It's important to recognize that these symptoms can also indicate other health issues, so it's advisable to consult healthcare professionals for accurate diagnosis and treatment. Managing chronic stress often requires a multifaceted approach, often involving a combination of somatic therapy and other treatment paths tailored to an individual's circumstance.

How to Move Forward

Recognizing the signs and symptoms of both trauma and chronic stress is crucial for several reasons, especially when considering the role of somatic therapy in treatment. Firstly, early recognition of these symptoms can lead to prompt intervention, which is often key to preventing more severe, long-term psychological and physical health issues. In the context of somatic therapy, understanding these signs is particularly important because this approach focuses on the physical manifestations of emotional and psychological distress. For instance, chronic muscle tension, a common physical symptom of both trauma and chronic stress, can be an entry point for somatic therapy. Through techniques like mindful movement and breathwork, somatic therapy addresses these physical symptoms, often the body's way of signaling unresolved emotional issues.

Moreover, recognizing these signs and symptoms can help individuals and therapists tailor the therapeutic approach to their specific needs. Somatic therapy is highly personalized; what works for one person may not work for another. Understanding the specific ways in which trauma or chronic stress manifests in an individual can guide the somatic therapist or, in this case, yourself in choosing the most effective techniques and approaches.

Furthermore, awareness of these symptoms empowers individuals to actively participate in their healing journey. Somatic therapy is about receiving treatment and learning to tune into one's body and understand its signals. By recognizing their symptoms, individuals can begin to make connections between their physical sensations and emotional states, a key step in the somatic healing process. This self-awareness fosters a deeper mind-body connection, enhancing the effectiveness of therapy and promoting long-term resilience and well-being.

In summary, recognizing the signs and symptoms of trauma and chronic stress is essential for timely and effective intervention. In somatic therapy, this awareness is the foundation upon which the therapy builds, guiding both the therapist and the individual in a collaborative process toward healing and recovery.

As we move forward, we'll look deeper into the brain-body nexus and see the neurobiology that makes somatic therapy possible.

Chapter 3

The Science Behind Somatic Healing

In this chapter, we'll review the intricate science underpinning somatic therapy. This study will help us reveal the complex interplay between the brain and the body. We will uncover how trauma affects not only our psychological state but also leaves indelible marks on our physical being.

Our first stop is the neurobiology of trauma, where we'll delve into the "Brain-Body Nexus." Here, we'll explore how traumatic experiences can alter the brain's structure and functioning, impacting everything from emotional regulation to physical health, something we briefly touched upon in the previous chapter. This section will help us appreciate the depth and breadth of trauma's impact and set the stage for understanding the necessity of a body-focused approach to healing.

Next, we transition into examining what makes somatic therapy possible. We'll investigate how somatic techniques – from mindful movement to breathwork – can reshape neural pathways. This segment will provide a fascinating look at how somatic therapy not only aids in emotional healing but also facilitates profound neurological changes, offering a beacon of hope for lasting recovery and resilience.

Finally, we will look at the body of research available and see if somatic therapy is a promising approach to mental healthcare. This section will ground our understanding in the latest findings, highlighting the effectiveness of somatic practices in healing trauma. By examining scientific studies and real-world evidence, we will solidify our understanding of somatic therapy as a legitimate and powerful tool in the healing arsenal.

As we traverse through this chapter, we will gain a deeper, scientifically grounded understanding of how somatic therapy operates and why it's an essential modality for those seeking to heal from trauma or chronic stress.

Neurobiology of Trauma: Unraveling the Brain-Body Nexus

The brain-body nexus in the context of trauma is a fascinating and complex area of study that underscores the deep interconnection between our mental processes and physical state. This nexus refers to how the brain and body communicate and influence each other, particularly in how trauma is experienced and processed.

When a traumatic event occurs, it activates the brain's stress response system. The amygdala, which plays a key role in processing emotions like fear and anxiety, signals the hypothalamus to initiate the body's fight-or-flight response. This leads to a cascade of physiological changes: the adrenal glands secrete stress hormones like cortisol and adrenaline, increase heart rate and blood pressure, and mobilize energy resources.

These immediate responses are the body's way of preparing to deal with a threat, but when trauma is severe, repeated, or ongoing, these systems can become dysregulated. The brain can get stuck in a state of heightened alertness, and the body remains in prolonged stress. This chronic activation can lead to various long-term effects on both the brain and the body. For instance, prolonged exposure to cortisol can alter brain function, particularly in areas like the hippocampus, which is involved in memory formation and stress regulation.

The brain-body nexus also involves how the body stores and remembers trauma. Trauma survivors might experience somatic symptoms – like unexplained pain, gastrointestinal problems, or heightened startle response – that don't have a clear physical cause. These are often the body's ways of expressing unresolved trauma. The body, in a sense, "remembers" the trauma and these memories are stored not just in the brain but also in the body's tissues and systems.

Furthermore, the brain-body connection in trauma is evident in how our bodily states can influence our emotional healing. For example, practices that promote relaxation and reduce physical tension can calm the brain and help regulate emotional responses. This is why therapies that focus on the body, like somatic therapy, can be particularly effective for trauma survivors.

BRAIN-BODY NEXUS ILLUSTRATED

Let's illustrate the brain-body nexus with a hypothetical anecdote:

Meet Emily, a dedicated paramedic working in emergency medical services for over a decade. One night, she responds to a particularly harrowing car accident. Although she performs her duties with her usual professionalism, the severity of the scene deeply affects her.

In the following weeks, Emily begins to notice changes in herself. Despite being a seasoned paramedic accustomed to stressful situations, she starts experiencing intense anxiety, especially when her pager goes off. Her heart races, her palms sweat, and she feels a sense of dread, even when responding to routine calls.

Physically, Emily starts having trouble sleeping. She's plagued by nightmares about the accident and finds herself waking up in a cold sweat. During her shifts, she notices her hands trembling, a new and unsettling development for her.

What Emily is experiencing is the brain-body nexus in action following her traumatic experience. Her brain, particularly her amygdala, has become hyper-vigilant, constantly on the lookout for danger. This heightened state of alert is triggering her body's stress response – even in situations that she used to handle with ease.

At the same time, her body is holding onto the trauma. The nightmares, the sweating, the tremors – these are all ways in which her body is expressing and responding to the unresolved trauma. Her physical reactions are not just random symptoms; they are deeply connected to her emotional state and the traumatic event she experienced.

Seeking help, Emily sees promise in somatic therapy. Through this therapy, she learns to tune into her body's signals. She starts practicing mindfulness and breathing exercises, which help calm her physiological stress response. Gradually, Emily begins to feel more in control. The trembling subsides, her sleep improves, and her anxiety becomes more manageable.

Emily's example illustrates the brain-body nexus in the context of trauma. It shows how the brain's response to trauma can manifest physically and how addressing these physical responses can, in turn, reverse the damage and aid in emotional healing.

KEY FEATURES OF THE BRAIN-BODY NEXUS SUMMARIZED

• **Trauma Affects Brain Function:** Traumatic experiences can cause changes in the brain, particularly in areas like the amygdala, hippocampus, and prefrontal cortex, which are involved in processing emotions, memory, and stress response.

- **Body's Stress Response:** The brain's reaction to trauma activates the body's fight-or-flight response, leading to physical changes like increased heart rate, heightened alertness, and the release of stress hormones.

- **Chronic Dysregulation:** Prolonged or repeated trauma can lead to a chronic state of heightened neurological and physiological arousal, disrupting normal brain and body functioning and potentially leading to various health issues.

- **Somatic Memory:** The body can "store" traumatic experiences, manifesting as physical symptoms or sensations seemingly unconnected to any current medical condition.

- **Mind-Body Connection in Healing:** Addressing the physical manifestations of trauma, such as through somatic therapy, can help regulate the body's stress response and facilitate emotional healing, illustrating the deep interconnectivity between the brain and the body.

Somatic Therapy's Influence on Neural Pathways

UNDERSTANDING NEUROPLASTICITY

Somatic therapy's connection with our neurobiology is rooted in neuroplasticity.

Neuroplasticity is a fundamental concept in neuroscience that refers to the brain's ability to change and adapt throughout an individual's life. This adaptability is a crucial aspect of how the brain develops from infancy through adulthood and how it recovers from injury.

One of the primary ways neuroplasticity manifests is through learning and experience. When we learn something or have new experiences, our brain forms new connections between neurons (nerve cells).

These connections, or synapses, are where communication between neurons occurs. Repeated experiences or practice can strengthen these connections, making the associated skill or knowledge more ingrained.

Secondly, neuroplasticity allows the brain to reorganize itself functionally and structurally in response to changes in the environment, behavior, neural processes, thinking, and emotions. For example, if one area of the brain is damaged, another area may adapt to take over some of its functions.

Moreover, although most neuron formation occurs during childhood, research has shown that neurogenesis, or the creation of new neurons, can happen in certain areas of the brain during adulthood, as well. This process is influenced by various factors, including physical activity, environmental enrichment, and learning.

Neuroplasticity is also a key factor in the brain's ability to recover from injuries. As we mentioned, post-injury, the brain can rewire itself and reassign certain functions to undamaged areas. Rehabilitation efforts, such as physical therapy, speech therapy, and cognitive exercises, leverage neuroplasticity to aid in recovery.

On the flip side, chronic stress and trauma can negatively affect neuroplasticity. They can lead to changes in brain structure and function, particularly in memory, emotional regulation, and executive functioning. However, positive interventions, such as therapy and stress management techniques, can help reverse these effects.

Finally, neuroplasticity is not just limited to childhood; it continues throughout life. The brain's ability to adapt and change offers opportunities for continued learning, cognitive development, and recovery from neurological conditions well into older age.

Understanding the brain's malleability has profound implications for therapies and treatments for various neurological and psychological conditions.

HOW SOMATIC THERAPY AFFECTS OUR NEUROBIOLOGY

Focusing on neuroplasticity, the influence of somatic therapy on our neurobiology becomes even more intriguing. Somatic therapy, with its emphasis on body awareness and physical sensations, engages the brain in a unique way. When individuals consciously focus on their bodily states and movements, they activate specific areas of the brain involved in sensory processing and emotional regulation. This activation is where neuroplasticity comes into play.

1. **Forming New Neural Connections:** Engaging in somatic practices like mindful movement or focused breathing can stimulate the formation of new neural pathways. For example, when practicing mindfulness, the brain's neural circuits associated with attention and sensory processing are engaged and strengthened.

2. **Rewiring Stress Responses:** Regular practice of somatic techniques can lead to changes in the areas of the brain responsible for the stress response, such as the amygdala and hippocampus. Repeating the body's relaxation response can help downregulate an overactive stress response system, rewiring the brain to react more calmly to stressors.

3. **Enhancing Emotional Integration:** Somatic therapy can facilitate better emotional integration by engaging the brain's limbic system, which is involved in emotion and memory processing. Through body-focused practices, individuals can form new, healthier associations with emotional experiences, particularly those related to trauma.

4. **Improving Self-Regulation and Awareness:** By increasing body awareness, somatic therapy strengthens the neural pathways related to interoception (explained later). This improvement can lead to better self-regulation as individuals become more attuned to their physiological responses to stress and emotions.

5. **Supporting Overall Brain Function:** Somatic practices can also support overall brain health and cognitive function. For instance, stress reduction and improved emotional regulation can enhance focus, memory, and cognitive clarity.

In essence, through the lens of neuroplasticity, somatic therapy is not just about managing symptoms; it's about fundamentally reshaping the brain's response to trauma and stress. By leveraging the brain's innate ability to adapt and change, somatic therapy offers a powerful tool for healing and personal transformation.

LONG-TERM EFFECTS ON NEUROLOGICAL HEALTH

Sustained involvement in somatic therapy can lead to enduring changes in brain structure and function. These changes have profound implications for long-term neurological health. For instance, enhanced emotional regulation can be attributed to strengthening the prefrontal cortex, the brain area responsible for decision-making and regulating emotions. This improved functioning can lead to better management of emotions and a reduced reactivity to stressors. Furthermore, by regularly invoking the body's relaxation response, there can be a reduction in the chronic activation of the stress response system. This leads to decreased symptoms associated with anxiety and stress, contributing to overall mental well-being.

These long-term changes can also impact other cognitive functions, such as memory, attention, and problem-solving skills, as these areas of the brain are interrelated. By fostering a state of reduced stress and heightened body-mind connection, somatic therapy can support cognitive health and resilience against age-related cognitive decline.

If you keep up some of the somatic practices we'll teach you even after your condition has subsided, the long-term approach can not only aid in immediate stress relief and trauma recovery but also contribute to a more resilient and adaptable brain, promoting sustained neurological health and wellness.

EXPLORING INTEROCEPTION

Interoception refers to our ability to sense and interpret the internal signals of our body, such as heart rate, hunger, thirst, and physical discomfort. It's crucial to how we experience and understand our emotions and bodily needs. With its focus on bodily sensations and movements, somatic therapy plays a significant role in enhancing this internal awareness.

Somatic therapy strengthens the neural pathways associated with interoceptive awareness by guiding individuals to pay close attention to their bodily sensations. This heightened awareness allows individuals to better understand and respond to their emotional and physical states. For example, recognizing the physical signs of stress or anxiety – like increased heart rate or muscle tension – can prompt techniques to mitigate these responses.

The improvement in interoceptive awareness also has a direct impact on emotional regulation. The insular cortex, a brain region involved in interoception, is also key in processing emotions. By enhancing interoception, somatic therapy can help better identify and manage emotions. For instance, being aware of a 'knot' in the stomach as a sign of anxiety can enable more effective coping strategies.

Furthermore, improved interoceptive awareness can lead to a deeper understanding of one's emotional and physical needs, fostering better self-care and overall well-being. It helps develop a more harmonious relationship with one's body, moving away from ignoring or misinterpreting bodily signals to a state of acknowledgment and responsiveness.

The role of interoception in somatic therapy is a vital component of its effectiveness and cannot be overlooked.

Research and Evidence: The Validity of Somatic Approaches

Does somatic therapy work? It's a genuine concern, of course. Especially when you've been dealing with mental anguish day in and day out without any respite. Well, empirical evidence points to its efficacy in many situations. Let's take a look at some of the available proof and some limitations in the study of somatic therapy.

EMPIRICAL STUDIES AND CLINICAL TRIALS

Over the years, numerous studies and clinical trials have focused on examining the effectiveness of somatic therapy techniques. These studies often involve participants with a history of trauma or chronic stress and measure various outcomes, such as reductions in symptoms of PTSD, anxiety, and depression. The findings generally indicate that somatic therapy significantly improves emotional regulation, stress management, and overall mental health.

NEUROSCIENTIFIC RESEARCH

Neuroscientific research provides insight into how somatic therapy impacts the brain. Brain imaging studies have shown that practices central to somatic therapy, like mindfulness and controlled breathing, can lead to changes in brain regions associated with stress, emotion regulation, and body awareness. These changes are evidence of the brain's neuroplasticity in action, reflecting its ability to adapt and rewire itself in response to somatic therapy.

COMPARISON WITH OTHER THERAPIES

Comparative studies that evaluate somatic therapy against other forms of treatment, such as cognitive-behavioral therapy (CBT) or medication, provide additional layers of understanding. While somatic therapy may not always be a standalone solution for everyone, research often shows it to be a valuable complementary approach, enhancing the effectiveness of other therapies or providing an alternative when traditional therapies have limited success.

QUALITATIVE RESEARCH AND CASE STUDIES

Beyond quantitative research, qualitative studies and case reports deepen our understanding of somatic therapy's impact. These studies, which often include detailed accounts of individual experiences, underscore the profound personal transformations that can occur through somatic practices, offering insights beyond numbers and data.

Since somatic therapy is a relatively new development, the body of research and evidence supporting somatic approaches is growing and becoming more robust. This research validates somatic therapy as an effective treatment option and deepens our understanding of the link between the mind, body, and health. As the field continues to evolve, further research will undoubtedly continue to shed light on somatic therapy's nuances and broader implications in mental health and well-being.

LIMITATIONS OF SOMATIC THERAPY RESEARCH

While increasingly recognized and utilized, somatic therapy has some limitations in terms of the breadth and depth of research compared to more traditional therapies like cognitive-behavioral therapy (CBT). While there is growing evidence supporting its effectiveness, particularly in the treatment of trauma and stress-related disorders, the body of research on somatic therapy is not as extensive as some other therapeutic approaches.

Several factors contribute to this problem:

1. **Methodological Challenges:** Somatic therapy encompasses a wide range of highly individualized techniques, making it challenging to study using traditional research methods. Standardized protocols used in research may not capture somatic therapy's nuanced and personalized nature.

2. **Emerging Field:** Somatic therapy is relatively newer as a formalized therapeutic approach than more established therapies. As a result, it has had less time to accumulate a substantial body of research.

3. **Lack of Large-Scale Studies:** Many studies on somatic therapy are small-scale or lack control groups, which are crucial for establishing efficacy in the scientific community. Large-scale, randomized controlled trials are needed to provide more definitive evidence of its effectiveness.

4. Qualitative vs. Quantitative Data: Much evidence supporting somatic therapy is qualitative, based on individual experiences and case studies. While this type of evidence is valuable in psychology, there is a need for more quantitative research to satisfy scientific standards of evidence.

5. Integration with Other Therapies: Somatic therapy is often used in conjunction with other treatment modalities, making it difficult to isolate its specific effects in research studies.

Despite these challenges, the research that does exist is positive and indicates the potential of somatic therapy in treating a range of conditions, particularly those related to trauma and chronic stress. Ongoing research efforts are crucial for further validating and understanding the effectiveness and mechanisms of somatic therapy, contributing to its broader acceptance and utilization in the mental health field.

IS SOMATIC THERAPY PROMISING?

Somatic therapy indeed holds considerable promise as a therapeutic approach, particularly for those grappling with the effects of trauma and chronic stress. At its heart, somatic therapy offers a profound recognition of the intricate bond between mind and body, a bond that is often overlooked in more traditional forms of therapy. This approach is especially hopeful for individuals who have found that talking about their experiences or understanding them cognitively isn't enough for healing. Somatic therapy provides an alternative path, one that involves tuning into the body's wisdom, listening to its signals, and gently working through the physical manifestations of emotional pain.

The promise of somatic therapy also lies in its empowering nature. It equips individuals with practical, body-based tools to self-regulate and manage symptoms, fostering a sense of autonomy in their healing journey. This empowerment can be particularly transformative for those who have felt helpless or trapped by their traumatic experiences or people who've felt tied up to clinics and therapy sessions.

Moreover, the growing body of research supporting somatic therapy adds to this hope. Emerging studies suggest that practices central to somatic therapy, like mindfulness and breathwork, can lead to positive changes in the brain and body, offering a scientific foundation for the healing that many experience.

For anyone navigating the challenging terrain of trauma and stress, somatic therapy shines as a beacon of hope. It acknowledges the deep scars that such experiences can leave, not just on the mind but also on the body. It offers a holistic path to recovery that is gentle, empowering, and grounded in the wisdom of one's own body. In the evolving landscape of mental health and healing, somatic therapy stands out as a promising avenue toward profound, lasting change.

Chapter Summary

We started by exploring the neurobiology of trauma and understanding how traumatic experiences impact our brain and body's intricate network. We then delved into how somatic therapy influences neural pathways, utilizing the brain's neuroplasticity to foster healing and recovery. Lastly, we examined the growing body of research and evidence supporting the validity of somatic approaches, highlighting their promise in mental health.

Through this exploration, we've gained insights into how somatic therapy addresses mental growth and recovery. This holistic approach, grounded in scientific understanding, offers a unique and effective pathway for healing from trauma and managing chronic stress.

As we close this chapter, we prepare to step into the next, where we will explore various types of somatic therapy modules. Each module presents its unique approach to healing, offering a range of techniques and practices that cater to different needs and preferences.

Chapter 4

Types of Somatic Therapy Modalities

As an overarching theme, we've established that somatic therapy targets the physical manifestations of psychological conditions. Still, there's a diversity of approaches or "modalities" within somatic therapy, and one may work out better for you than the other, or you may even decide to opt for a combination approach.

First, we'll begin with Body-Centered Therapies, where we delve into therapies emphasizing a deep connection with the physical body. These practices are grounded in the belief that we can access deeper emotional and psychological insights by engaging the body, leading to transformative healing experiences.

Next, we'll unravel Sensorimotor Psychotherapy. This approach integrates the body's sensorimotor responses with traditional psychotherapy. It's a modality that acknowledges the body's role in storing and expressing emotions and uses bodily sensations and movements as entry points for psychological exploration and healing.

Lastly, we'll engage with Dance/Movement Therapy. Here, as the name suggests, we discover the therapeutic power of movement and dance. This modality harnesses the body's expressive potential, using dance and movement as tools for emotional expression, self-discovery, and psychological healing.

Each of these modalities showcases the versatility and efficacy of somatic therapy, offering different lenses through which to view and engage with the healing process. As we break down these therapeutic models, we will gain a deeper appreciation for the myriad ways the body can be a vessel for healing and growth. Each modality serves a unique role; let's see how.

Embodied Practices: Body-Centered Therapies

These therapies are founded on the principle that the body is not just a reflection of our mental and emotional states but an active participant in the experience and processing of these states.

Embodied practices in therapy focus on heightening body awareness and engaging with the physical sensations, movements, and postures that arise during therapy. This approach is rooted in the understanding that emotional and psychological issues often manifest physically, through muscle tension, breath patterns, or other bodily responses.

Key aspects of embodied practices include mindfulness exercises, where clients are guided to pay attention to their bodily sensations in the present moment. Techniques such as guided imagery, grounding exercises, and focused breathing are also commonly used to help clients reconnect with their bodies, often leading to insights and emotional releases that might not emerge through traditional talk therapy alone.

Body-centered therapies often incorporate movement – not necessarily structured exercises but organic movements that arise from tuning into the body's natural impulses. This movement can be a powerful tool for expressing emotions that are hard to articulate with words and can lead to a greater sense of freedom and release.

By focusing on the physical form, these therapies aim to break down the barriers between mind and body, creating a more integrated sense of self. Clients learn to recognize and respond to their physical cues, leading to improved emotional regulation and a deeper understanding of their emotional experiences.

TYPES OF BODY-CENTERED TECHNIQUES

Here are examples of various types of embodied practices that fall under the category of body-centered therapies, illustrating the diverse ways in which these therapies engage the body in the healing process:

1. **Hakomi Method:** This mindfulness-based approach utilizes guided self-study within a therapeutic setting. It explores the client's internal experiences, using physical sensations and emotions as entry points to uncover unconscious beliefs and patterns.

2. **Feldenkrais Method:** This method involves gentle movements and focused attention to improve movement and enhance human functioning. It's about learning new movement patterns and awareness to increase physical comfort and mental ease.

3. **Alexander Technique:** This technique teaches people how to stop using unnecessary muscular and mental tension levels during their everyday activities. It is often used to improve posture, relieve chronic pain, and reduce stress.

4. **Bioenergetic Analysis:** This therapy combines work with the body and mind to help people resolve their emotional problems and realize their potential for pleasure and joy in living. It involves

exercises to release chronic muscular tensions, enhance body awareness, and support emotional expression.

5. **Rolfing Structural Integration:** Focusing on the body's alignment and structural balance, Rolfing involves manipulating the connective tissues to release, realign, and balance the whole body, thus potentially resolving discomfort, reducing compensations, and alleviating pain.

These examples showcase the range of body-centered therapies available, each with its unique focus and methodology, but all sharing the common thread of using the body as a key element in the therapeutic process.

Sensorimotor Psychotherapy: Engaging Body and Mind

Sensorimotor psychotherapy, a term rooted in the fields of neuroscience and psychology, refers to a therapeutic approach that integrates sensorimotor processing with cognitive and emotional processing in the treatment of trauma and stress-related disorders. The term "sensorimotor" itself combines two key components: "sensory," relating to sensation or the senses, and "motor," meaning movement.

This approach is based on the understanding that traumatic experiences can become embedded in our bodies. Trauma and chronic stress can disrupt the body's natural sensorimotor responses, leading to dysregulation in how we process and respond to sensory information and physically react to emotional stimuli.

Sensorimotor psychotherapy focuses on the body's role in the individual's psychological experiences. It pays close attention to the physiological responses accompanying emotional and cognitive processes, particularly those activated when recalling or discussing traumatic events. Doing so aims to help clients become more aware of their bodily sensations and movements and use this awareness as a gateway to process and resolve traumatic experiences.

It utilizes the body (sensorimotor experiences) as a primary entry point in therapy, alongside traditional talk therapy techniques, to address the psychological effects of trauma and promote holistic healing.

WHAT DOES SENSORIMOTOR FAILURE LOOK LIKE?

When stress or trauma overwhelms an individual, it can lead to a phenomenon known as sensorimotor failure, where the body's natural ability to process and respond to sensory and motor signals gets disrupted. Imagine being in a constant state of high alert, where even the slightest noise or movement puts you on edge. This is what life can feel like for someone experiencing sensorimotor failure due to trauma or chronic stress. Their startle response is dialed up to the maximum, making everyday surprises feel like significant threats.

This heightened state of vigilance is just one aspect. Some individuals might feel strangely detached from their bodies as if they're floating through life without fully experiencing physical sensations. This dissociation can make them unaware of their bodily needs and responses, adding a layer of complexity to their experience of the world.

Movement and coordination can also become casualties of this condition. Tasks that once felt natural and effortless might now seem clumsy or uncoordinated. Imagine feeling like your body isn't quite keeping up with what your brain asks it to do. Alongside this, the body might hold onto tension like a tightly wound spring, particularly in the shoulders and neck, leading to persistent aches and pains.

Individuals might sometimes experience a 'freeze' response in stressful situations. It's as if their body hits a pause button, leaving them stuck and unable to move. Breathing patterns can become irregular too, with breaths either coming too fast and shallow or seeming to stop altogether.

Even the digestive system isn't immune to the effects of sensorimotor failure. The turmoil within can manifest as stomachaches, nausea, or other gastrointestinal discomforts, further indicating the body's distress under the weight of stress or trauma.

Sensorimotor failure disrupts the harmonious communication between body and mind, creating a range of challenges that go beyond the psychological symptoms of trauma and stress. It's a vivid reminder of the intricate connection between our mental and physical states and underscores the need for therapeutic approaches that address both aspects in tandem for holistic healing.

SENSORIMOTOR THERAPY AT PLAY

Let's explore how sensorimotor psychotherapy works through a simple narrative:

Imagine Anna, a young woman who has been struggling with anxiety and emotional numbness, a lingering effect of a car accident she experienced a year ago. She decided to try sensorimotor psychotherapy after traditional talk therapy had limited success in alleviating her symptoms.

In her first session, Anna's therapist explains that this approach will involve not just talking about her experiences but also paying attention to her body's responses when recalling her traumatic memory. The therapist assures her that she is in a safe space and has control over the process.

As they start talking about the accident, Anna feels tense, and her breathing becomes shallow. Her therapist gently notices this and asks Anna to focus on these physical sensations. Anna realizes she's clenching her fists, and her heart is racing — physical reactions she hadn't been conscious of before.

Her therapist guides her to notice these sensations without judgment and then leads her through breathing exercises. As Anna breathes deeply, she feels her fists slowly unclenching. Her therapist then asks her to gently move her arms, mimicking the motion of releasing something she's been holding onto.

Throughout the sessions, Anna learns to tune into her body's signals — the tightening of her muscles, changes in her breath, and the feeling of heaviness in her limbs. She starts understanding how her body has been holding onto the trauma of the accident and begins to work through these physical sensations.

Gradually, Anna notices changes. Her anxiety lessens, and she feels more in touch with her emotions. By focusing on her body's responses and learning to regulate them, she's able to process the trauma in a way that words alone couldn't reach. She's actively reconnecting her mind with her body, learning the language of her physical responses, and using this awareness to heal.

This narrative demonstrates the essence of sensorimotor psychotherapy — an approach that integrates the body's sensorimotor responses with cognitive and emotional healing.

Dance/Movement Therapy: Expressive Pathways to Healing

When we refer to "dance" in the context of dance/movement therapy, we're talking about a therapeutic practice that goes beyond the traditional concept of dance as performance or entertainment. In dance/movement therapy, dance is a medium for emotional expression, psychological healing, and personal growth. It encompasses a broad range of movement styles and is not confined to any specific type or genre of dance.

In this therapeutic approach, "dance" is about using body movements, ranging from subtle to dynamic, as a form of nonverbal communication and self-expression. The movements in dance/movement therapy are often improvisational and spontaneous, allowing individuals to explore and express their inner feelings and emotions through their bodies. This includes rhythmic movements, free-form dancing, or simple gestures and postures.

The idea is to connect the mind and body to promote emotional release, self-awareness, and healing. The movements in dance/

movement therapy are used as tools to enhance an individual's emotional, cognitive, physical, and social integration. It is an embodied practice emphasizing the interconnectedness of the body, mind, and spirit.

In summary, "dance" in this context is not about learning choreographed steps or performing but rather about using movement as a therapeutic tool for emotional and psychological healing. It's an inclusive, accessible form of therapy that acknowledges and harnesses the power of physical expression as a pathway to mental health and well-being.

WHEN OUR BODIES COMMUNICATE

Expanding on the role of nonverbal communication in dance/movement therapy, it's crucial to recognize how this form of therapy harnesses the power of body language and physical expression as fundamental tools for healing and self-discovery. In dance/movement therapy, nonverbal communication goes beyond mere gestures or movements; it becomes a language in its own right, offering a means of expressing emotions and experiences that might be difficult to articulate in words.

1. **Expression Beyond Words:** For many individuals, especially those who have experienced trauma or who find verbal expression challenging, traditional talk therapy can be limiting. Dance/movement therapy provides an alternative medium. Through movement, clients can express complex and deep-seated emotions that are hard to verbalize. This could include expressing sadness, joy, anger, or fear through dance and movement.

2. **Body Language as Insight:** Our body language often reflects our subconscious thoughts and feelings. In dance/movement therapy, therapists are trained to observe and interpret these nonverbal cues. This insight can guide the therapy process, helping clients explore and understand their emotional states more deeply.

3. **Healing Through Movement:** Movement itself can be therapeutic. It's an expression of emotions and a way to work through and

release them. For example, rhythmic movements can be soothing and help regulate emotions, while expansive, expressive movements can empower and release pent-up energy or tension.

4. **Building a Body-Mind Connection:** Dance/movement therapy fosters a stronger connection between the body and mind. As clients become more attuned to their physical expressions and movements, they often gain greater awareness of their emotional and mental states. This heightened body-mind connection can lead to improved self-awareness and emotional regulation.

5. **Creating a Safe Space for Expression:** For those with difficulty with trust or vulnerability, the nonverbal aspect of dance/movement therapy can create a safer space for expression. It allows individuals to communicate and process their feelings without the pressure or exposure that can come with verbal disclosure.

In essence, the role of nonverbal communication in dance/ movement therapy is multifaceted and powerful. It provides a unique and effective way for individuals to express themselves, process their emotions, and embark on a healing journey, often reaching places that words alone cannot access. This approach is particularly beneficial in addressing issues deeply embedded in the psyche, offering a path to healing that is both physically embodied and emotionally liberating.

Chapter Summary

In this chapter, we delved into the diverse and dynamic field of somatic therapy modalities, each offering unique approaches to healing by integrating body and mind.

We began with Body-Centered Therapies, exploring therapies that focus on deepening bodily awareness and using physical sensations as gateways to emotional and psychological insight. These practices underscore the principle that our bodies hold and express emotions, offering a path to physically engaged and emotionally profound healing.

Next, we examined Sensorimotor Psychotherapy. This approach integrates the body's sensorimotor responses with cognitive and emotional processes, which is particularly effective in treating trauma. It emphasizes the role of the body in storing and expressing emotions, using bodily sensations and movements to access and heal psychological wounds.

Finally, we explored Dance/Movement Therapy, where dance and movement are therapeutic tools. This modality leverages the expressive power of the body, using dance and movement for emotional expression, self-discovery, and psychological healing. It's an approach that highlights the transformative potential of physical expression in mental health.

KEY TAKEAWAYS:

1. **Body as a Gateway to Healing:** Each modality emphasizes the body as a central element in the therapeutic process, recognizing its role in expressing and processing emotions.

2. **Diverse Techniques for Diverse Needs:** The range of somatic therapy modalities offers various pathways to healing, catering to different preferences and therapeutic needs.

3. **Holistic Approach:** These therapies underscore a holistic approach to mental health, integrating the physical, emotional, and psychological aspects of the individual.

4. **Empowerment and Self-Awareness:** Somatic therapies empower individuals by enhancing body awareness and providing tools for self-regulation and emotional processing.

5. **Nonverbal Expression:** Techniques like dance/movement therapy highlight the importance of nonverbal expression, offering alternatives for those who find traditional talk therapy challenging.

Next up, we'll look at some case studies and stories of individuals who stand as a testament to conquering your invisible wounds through somatic therapy.

Chapter 5

Real-Life Experiments and Stories in Somatic Therapy

The go-to way to test a therapy's effectiveness is to see if it has worked for others, and that's exactly what we intend to present in this chapter. Testimonials bring a human element to the understanding of somatic therapy, offering narratives that resonate personally and provide a vivid illustration of its effects.

They provide compelling evidence of the therapy's effectiveness, supplementing clinical data with the richness of individual experiences. Through these stories, we gain diverse perspectives on how somatic therapy is experienced and beneficial, reflecting its adaptability to various personal contexts.

Keeping the scientific aspect aside, more importantly, these narratives offer inspiration and hope, encouraging others who might be considering somatic therapy. They also demystify the therapy process, providing insights into its practical application and the real-world healing journey. Let's look at some case studies, personal testimonials, and practical narratives to see how the somatic path turns out.

Disclaimer: To protect the right to privacy, names and personal details may have been changed.

Case Studies: Experiences of Individuals in Somatic Therapy

WHAT IS A CASE STUDY?

You might have heard the term "case study" get thrown around a lot when eloquent speakers start gunning facts during public speeches. The reason is pure and simple: it gives credibility to the argument. So, what exactly is a case study?

A case study is like a detailed story about a person's experiences, especially when it comes to their journey through something challenging, like an illness or a tough situation. Imagine you're reading a story about someone named Alex who's going through a difficult time, maybe feeling anxious or having trouble coping with something that happened in their past.

In this story, you learn all about Alex – what they're struggling with, how they feel, what they've tried to feel better, and who's helping them, like a therapist or a doctor. The case study would tell you about Alex's specific methods or treatments, like talking to a therapist, doing some special exercises, or maybe trying a new kind of therapy.

As the story goes on, you see how Alex changes and hopefully starts to feel better. You learn about what worked for them, what didn't, and how they navigated the ups and downs of their journey. It's like getting a behind-the-scenes look at someone's path to overcoming challenges.

So, a case study is a deep dive into people's experiences when that process is documented in a clinical/academic setting. It's a way for us to learn about different problems people face and how they can be solved, giving us valuable insights that we might apply to help others in similar situations. It's like learning from someone else's story to understand more about a particular issue and what might help.

TYPES OF CASE STUDIES COMMONLY ASSOCIATED WITH SOMATIC THERAPY

Performing case studies in the psychological realm is tricky since unique life circumstances, experiences, predispositions, biases, and outcomes shape each participant's condition. Naturally, the results of the case study are affected. Still, academia cannot rest. We have to perform several case studies that factor different elements into account and arrive at an average sum of the findings to reach a level of certainty.

These examples represent common scenarios where somatic therapy has been applied and the outcomes that have been observed:

1. **Trauma Recovery:** A common focus of somatic therapy case studies is individuals recovering from trauma. These studies often detail the client's initial symptoms (such as PTSD, anxiety, or dissociation), the specific somatic techniques used (like grounding exercises or mindful movement), and the progress made over time, including reduced symptoms and improved emotional regulation.

2. **Chronic Pain Management:** Some case studies explore somatic therapy for chronic pain conditions. These might describe clients who have struggled with long-term pain, the somatic approaches used to address both the physical sensations and the emotional aspects of living with pain, and the outcomes, such as reduced pain levels and improved quality of life.

3. **Stress and Anxiety Reduction:** Case studies often examine clients dealing with high levels of stress or anxiety. They typically outline the client's experience with stress or anxiety, the body-centered methods employed in therapy (like breathwork or sensorimotor psychotherapy), and the results, which might include lower stress levels, enhanced coping skills, and greater overall well-being.

4. **Overcoming Childhood Abuse or Neglect:** Somatic therapy is also applied in cases of childhood abuse or neglect. These case studies usually detail the client's background, how the trauma has manifested in their adult life, the somatic methods used in therapy, and the healing journey, often highlighting improved emotional processing and a stronger sense of self.

5. **Attachment and Relationship Issues:** Some case studies focus on individuals with attachment disorders or relationship issues stemming from their developmental years. These studies might describe how somatic therapy helped clients understand and address their relational patterns and their progress in forming healthier relationships.

6. **Dance/Movement Therapy in Special Populations:** In the context of dance/movement therapy, case studies might describe its application in special populations, such as elderly patients with dementia, children with developmental disorders, or individuals with physical disabilities, showcasing the unique benefits of movement-based therapy in these groups.

Each case study typically provides insights into the therapeutic process, the client-therapist dynamics, the challenges encountered, and the strategies used to overcome them. They serve as valuable resources for understanding somatic therapy's practical applications and effectiveness in real-world settings.

A CAR ACCIDENT SURVIVOR'S RECOVERY THROUGH SOMATIC THERAPY

Let's focus on the prima-donna of our book, trauma. Without naming them, this individual was a survivor of a car accident, an event that left them grappling with severe anxiety and flashbacks. These reactions were particularly triggered by specific stimuli related to the accident: the sight of cars and loud noises resembling the crash. These triggers would catapult the survivor back into the traumatic moment, overwhelming them with intense fear and anxiety. This is a common symptom of post-traumatic stress disorder (PTSD), where certain cues can evoke vivid, often distressing, memories of a traumatic event.

To address these challenges, the survivor turned to somatic therapy. This form of therapy is particularly suited to treating trauma because it focuses on the body's responses as well as the mind's reactions. In their therapy sessions, the individual was encouraged to tune into their body's reactions when recalling the trauma or when exposed to triggering stimuli.

Through this process, they became more aware of how their body was holding onto the trauma. This awareness was the first step in learning to manage and eventually alleviate the physical symptoms associated with their PTSD. The therapy involved working with these bodily sensations, acknowledging them, and using various techniques to help release the stored trauma.

Gradually, the individual learned to work through their body's responses, releasing the trapped energy and fear lodged in their physical self since the accident. As they progressed through therapy, they noticed a significant decrease in both the frequency and intensity of their anxiety and flashbacks.

Ultimately, somatic therapy allowed the survivor to regain a sense of safety and ease in their everyday life. They were able to move past the immediate and overwhelming bodily responses to their trauma triggers, finding a new sense of stability and calm in situations that previously would have been debilitating.

This case study highlights the effectiveness of somatic therapy in addressing the physical manifestations of trauma. It demonstrates how integrating the body into the healing process can lead to profound improvements in mental health and well-being.

FINDINGS

The case study, focusing on somatic therapy after a traumatic car accident, yielded the following key findings:

- **Severe Anxiety and Flashbacks:** The survivor suffered from intense anxiety and flashbacks triggered by stimuli associated with the car accident.

- **Somatic Therapy Approach:** The individual underwent somatic therapy, focusing on the body's responses to traumatic events.

- **Body Awareness:** Through therapy, the survivor learned to recognize and work with physical sensations linked to their trauma.

- **Release of Trauma:** The therapy facilitated the release of trapped energy and fear stored in the body since the accident.

- **Reduction in Symptoms:** A significant decrease was observed in both the frequency and intensity of the survivor's anxiety and flashbacks.

- **Regained Sense of Safety:** Post-therapy, the individual could reclaim a sense of safety and comfort in their daily life, indicating successful trauma processing and management.

Overcoming Childhood Abuse Through Somatic Therapy

How about something that has deeper roots than a recent car accident? Let's call our survivor Jordan.

Jordan, who endured childhood abuse, carried the emotional and psychological aftermath into adulthood. This history manifested in deep feelings of shame, a sense of disconnection from others, and a distrust in his own body.

Seeking healing, Jordan turned to somatic therapy. This therapeutic approach focused on body awareness and interpreting physical sensations as reflections of emotional states.

Through therapy, Jordan gradually began to reconnect with his body, a relationship that had been strained by past trauma. The therapy sessions involved mindful awareness of bodily sensations and movements, which allowed Jordan to explore and release emotions that had been stored and unacknowledged for years.

A significant part of the healing process for Jordan was developing self-compassion and self-acceptance. This was crucial in rebuilding a sense of self-worth and personal agency.

The outcome of the therapy was transformative for Jordan. He reported a newfound sense of resilience and strength, key to their long-term recovery and well-being. The therapy helped Jordan reclaim a sense of control and establish a more harmonious relationship with their body and emotions.

FINDINGS

Here are the key findings from the case study of Jordan, who underwent somatic therapy for childhood abuse trauma:

- **Background of Trauma:** The individual had a history of childhood abuse, which led to deep emotional and psychological scars, manifesting as shame, disconnection, and a distrust of their body.

- **Engagement in Somatic Therapy:** They sought healing through somatic therapy, focusing on reconnecting with their body and understanding its sensations as reflections of their emotional state.

- **Process of Reconnection:** The therapy facilitated a gradual reconnection with their body, helping them to safely explore and release stored emotions, often repressed due to the trauma.

- **Development of Self-Compassion:** A significant aspect of the therapy was the development of self-compassion and self-acceptance, crucial for rebuilding self-worth and agency after experiencing abuse.

- **Transformative Outcome:** The individual experienced a transformative healing process, reclaiming control over their body and emotions and developing a stronger sense of self.

- **Enhanced Resilience and Strength:** Post-therapy, they reported a newfound sense of resilience and strength, essential for long-term recovery and well-being.

Personal Testimonials: Stories of Triumph and Transformation

DIFFERENCE BETWEEN PERSONAL TESTIMONIAL AND CASE STUDY

The difference between a case study and a personal testimonial lies in their focus and presentation. A case study is an objective, comprehensive analysis, typically authored by professionals or researchers. It delves into a client's background, diagnosis, treatment, and outcomes, often incorporating data and documented evidence. Case studies provide a clinical perspective and are invaluable as educational tools, helping practitioners understand complex situations and therapeutic techniques.

On the other hand, a personal testimonial is a subjective narrative that highlights an individual's experience and emotional journey. Testimonials focus on the emotional impact and personal insights gained, offering a story relatable to a wider audience. While they may not include detailed clinical information or the nuances of the therapeutic process, testimonials are powerful in their emotional resonance, making them effective for advocacy and connecting with people on a personal level.

Both case studies and testimonials are crucial in understanding therapeutic interventions, but they cater to different needs – one offers detailed professional insight, the other provides a relatable human experience.

TESTAMENTS TO THE EFFICACY OF SOMATIC THERAPY

JAMES'S JOURNEY

"Before I started somatic therapy, I was constantly battling anxiety and felt a profound disconnect from my own body. Somatic therapy taught me how to tune into my body's signals and effectively release built-up tension. This journey has transformed my daily life; I now experience a sense of groundedness and presence that was previously missing."

ANNA'S REFLECTION

"Participating in a culturally sensitive somatic therapy group was life changing. It addressed the deep-seated trauma I had experienced related to racial issues. The safe and understanding environment the group and facilitators created allowed for profound healing that I couldn't have achieved otherwise."

ELENA'S INSIGHT

"When I began my training in somatic experiencing, I thought I would be learning to help broken people. But this experience opened my eyes to the resilience and beauty of the human spirit. Witnessing our collective ability to support, empathize, and heal together has filled me with hope and a newfound love for the human experience."

MICHAEL'S TRANSFORMATION

"Entering somatic therapy, I felt like a shadow of myself, burdened by past traumas. Through the sessions, I gradually learned to reconnect with my body and emotions in a way I never thought possible. It's as if I've rediscovered myself, gaining tools to manage my emotions and a newfound sense of inner peace. I'm more resilient and emotionally balanced now, and it's truly changed my life."

LAURA'S EXPERIENCE

"Somatic therapy was a revelation for me. Struggling with chronic stress, I found in it a sanctuary where I could learn to listen to my body. The therapy sessions were a journey of self-discovery, teaching me how to calm my mind and release physical tension.

I've emerged from this experience not just with reduced stress levels, but with a deeper appreciation and understanding of my own body and mind."

Based on real experiences, these accounts capture the essence of somatic therapy's transformative impact on individuals from various backgrounds, emphasizing its role in fostering emotional regulation, self-awareness, and resilience.

Applying Somatic Techniques in Daily Life: A Practical Roadmap

A practical application of somatic therapy typically follows a progressive roadmap, guiding individuals through various stages of self-awareness, healing, and growth. Here's what this journey might look like:

WEEKS 1-4: INITIAL ASSESSMENT AND BUILDING TRUST

• **Initial Sessions:** The process begins with an assessment where the therapist learns about the individual's background, challenges, and goals. This stage is crucial for building a foundation of trust and understanding.

• **Setting Intentions:** Together, the therapist and the individual set intentions and goals for the therapy, aligning expectations and establishing a clear direction.

WEEKS 5-8: DEVELOPING BODY AWARENESS

• **Introducing Body Awareness:** The individual is introduced to practices that heighten body awareness. This may include exercises focusing on breathing, noticing bodily sensations, and exploring movement.

- **Recognizing Patterns:** The individual starts to recognize patterns in how their body responds to stress, emotions, and trauma. This awareness is the first step in re-establishing a connection between the body and mind.

WEEKS 9-16: PROCESSING AND RELEASING EMOTIONS

- **Working Through Trauma:** As the individual becomes more attuned to their body, they begin to process and release emotions and trauma stored in the body. This might involve specific movements, postures, or exercises to release tension and trauma.

- **Emotional Regulation:** The individual learns techniques to regulate their emotional responses, using their newfound body awareness to manage stress and anxiety.

WEEKS 17-24: INTEGRATION AND EMPOWERMENT

- **Integrating Experiences:** The therapist helps the individual integrate their experiences and insights into daily life. This might involve developing routines or practices that incorporate somatic exercises.

- **Empowerment:** The individual gains tools and skills to manage their emotional and physical well-being independently, fostering a sense of empowerment and autonomy.

MONTHS 6-12: ADVANCED PRACTICES AND DEEPENING UNDERSTANDING

- **Deepening Practices:** As the individual progresses, they might engage in more advanced somatic practices, exploring deeper levels of body awareness and emotional processing.

- **Holistic Understanding:** The individual develops a holistic understanding of how their thoughts, emotions, and bodily sensations are interconnected, leading to a more integrated sense of self.

MONTHS 12 AND BEYOND: ONGOING GROWTH AND MAINTENANCE

• **Continued Practice:** Somatic therapy often becomes an ongoing practice, with the individual continuing to use the techniques they've learned to maintain their well-being and manage future challenges.

• **Further Exploration:** The individual might explore other complementary practices or deepen their somatic work as part of their growth journey.

Let's present a scenario illustrating someone following the somatic therapy roadmap:

MEET EMILY:

Weeks 1-4: Emily, dealing with chronic stress and anxiety, starts somatic therapy. She and her therapist discuss her goals and challenges in the first few sessions. She learns basic body awareness exercises.

Weeks 5-8: Emily notices how her body responds to stress – her tense shoulders, shallow breathing, or heart palpitations. She practices exercises that help her become more aware of these physical responses.

Weeks 9-16: Emily starts to work through the emotions tied to her stress. She uses body-focused techniques to release pent-up emotions. She learns strategies to regulate her emotional responses, like deep breathing, when overwhelmed.

Weeks 17-24: Emily works on integrating her therapy experiences into daily life. She establishes morning routines that include mindful movement and breathing exercises. She feels more empowered, using these techniques when she feels anxious.

Months 6-12: As Emily continues therapy, she delves deeper into somatic practices. She explores more complex exercises that help her understand the connection between her mind and body, leading to greater self-awareness and emotional insight.

Months 12 and Beyond: A year into therapy, Emily uses somatic techniques regularly to manage her stress and maintain her mental health. She meets with her therapist occasionally to refine her techniques and address new challenges, continuing her journey of personal growth and well-being.

In Emily's case, the somatic therapy roadmap has been a transformative journey, helping her manage her immediate symptoms and foster a deeper understanding and connection with her body, leading to long-term benefits in her overall quality of life.

This roadmap is a general guide and can vary depending on the individual's unique needs and circumstances. Somatic therapy is a personalized process, adapting to each person's compass for healing and self-discovery.

With the foundation laid, the basics of somatic therapy explained, and the roadmap established up until this point, you can take the first step and start your healing journey with the next section.

PART 2

Starting Your Healing Journey

Chapter 6

Getting Started with Somatic Therapy

Now, we turn to practical guidance on beginning somatic therapy. Some of the most dominant contributors to your effective recovery will be the kind of therapist you opt for, the support system you build for yourself, and the intentions you commit to on your recovery goals.

We'll first examine some important considerations when selecting a therapist. This involves understanding what to look for in a therapist or practitioner, considering factors like qualifications, experience, and personal compatibility, and the things that should set off sirens in your mind. It's about finding a professional who not only has the expertise but also resonates with your healing journey.

Healing is not a solitary journey; it flourishes in a supportive environment. Next, we'll offer strategies to build a support network, encompassing friends, family, community resources, and peer groups. It's about creating a nurturing ecosystem that encourages and sustains your healing process.

Finally, we'll discuss setting the right healing intentions based on your condition. This is about defining your goals and expectations for therapy. It involves identifying what you wish to achieve, understanding the steps involved, and recognizing the milestones. Setting clear intentions is a powerful way to stay focused and motivated throughout your therapeutic journey.

As we navigate through this chapter, our goal is to equip you with the knowledge and resources to confidently step into the world of somatic therapy, and hopefully, you'll be quickly on your way to a speedy recovery.

Finding the Right Therapist or Practitioner: Factors to Consider

HALLMARKS OF A SOMATIC THERAPIST

A somatic therapist stands out from other psychology therapists through their unique focus on the interconnectedness of the body and mind.

While traditional psychology therapists often concentrate on cognitive and emotional aspects – thoughts, feelings, and behaviors – somatic therapists bring the body to the therapeutic process's forefront. They operate on the understanding that emotional and psychological issues can manifest physically, and thus, addressing the body can be key to healing the mind. This perspective involves a holistic approach, where a therapist might often combine body-centered techniques with sub-conscious exploration.

Somatic therapists use techniques that involve movement, touch, breathwork, and body awareness exercises alongside talk therapy.

They are trained to notice subtle bodily responses and help clients become aware of their own physical sensations as they relate to emotional experiences.

FACTORS TO CONSIDER

When considering a somatic therapist, evaluating several key factors is important to ensure you find a practitioner who is well-suited to your needs and goals. Here are some considerations:

1. **Qualifications and Training:** Check the therapist's educational background and training in somatic therapy. Look for certifications or specialized training in somatic practices to ensure they have the necessary skills and knowledge.

2. **Experience:** Consider their experience, particularly with issues similar to yours. Experience in treating specific conditions like trauma, anxiety, or chronic pain can be beneficial.

3. **Therapeutic Approach:** Somatic therapy encompasses various techniques. Inquire about the therapist's approach and techniques and see if they align with your preferences and comfort level.

4. **Compatibility:** You must feel comfortable and safe with the therapist. This can be gauged through initial consultations or interactions. The therapeutic relationship plays a significant role in the effectiveness of therapy.

5. **Location and Accessibility:** Consider the therapist's location and whether it's convenient for you. Also, check if they offer remote sessions if you require them.

6. **Cost and Insurance:** Understand the cost of therapy and whether it fits your budget. Also, check if your insurance covers somatic therapy and if the therapist accepts your insurance.

7. **Personal Goals and Expectations:** Reflect on what you hope to achieve through somatic therapy and discuss these goals with potential therapists to see if they can meet your expectations.

8. **Specialization:** Some therapists might specialize in areas like dance/movement therapy, trauma-focused somatic therapy, etc. Choose one whose specialization aligns with your needs.

9. **Consultation Session:** Many therapists offer a first consultation session, which can be a good opportunity to assess compatibility and approach before committing.

Considering these factors can help you make an informed decision and choose a somatic therapist who is right for you, facilitating a more effective and comfortable therapeutic experience.

RED FLAGS TO AVOID

Identifying red flags in a somatic therapist is crucial for ensuring a safe therapeutic zone. Here are some warning signs to be aware of:

1. **Lack of Professional Boundaries:** A therapist should always maintain professional boundaries. Overstepping these is a significant red flag, whether through inappropriate personal disclosures, physical contact beyond what is therapeutically necessary, or blurring the lines between a professional and personal relationship.

2. **Disregarding Client Comfort:** A somatic therapist should always respect your comfort levels, especially with physical exercises or touch. If they ignore your discomfort or push you to engage in inappropriate or distressing activities, that's a concern.

3. **Unwillingness to Discuss Qualifications:** A reputable therapist will be transparent about their qualifications and training. If they are evasive or unwilling to discuss their credentials, that's a red flag.

4. **Guaranteeing Quick Fixes:** Be wary of therapists who promise quick fixes or instant results. Healing and therapy are typically gradual processes, and such promises can be unrealistic and misleading.

5. **Lack of Clear Communication:** The therapist should clearly communicate the therapy plan, goals, and techniques. If they are consistently vague or unclear, leaving you confused about the therapy process, that's a problem.

6. **Dismissive of Client's Concerns:** A good therapist listens and validates your concerns. If they are dismissive or belittling of your feelings or experiences, it shows a lack of empathy and professionalism.

7. **Unprofessional Conduct:** This includes any behavior that is unethical or unprofessional, such as frequent cancellations, being routinely late to sessions, or mishandling private information.

8. **Making the Sessions Unprofessionally Personal:** Therapy should focus on you, the client. If the therapist frequently shifts the focus to their issues or experiences, it can detract from your therapy.

9. **Lack of Progress or Negative Effects:** While progress can sometimes be slow, if you consistently feel worse after sessions or see no improvement over an extended period, it might indicate that the therapeutic approach is ineffective.

10. **Pressure to Continue Therapy:** The decision to continue or stop therapy should always be in your hands. If a therapist pressures you to continue against your wishes, it's a red flag.

If you encounter any of these red flags, it may be advisable to reconsider continuing therapy with that practitioner and possibly seek a second opinion or a different therapist.

THE POWER OF REVIEWS AND TESTIMONIALS

The power of testimonials when considering a somatic therapist lies in their ability to bring the therapist's work to life through the eyes of those who have experienced it firsthand. Imagine sitting down with a friend who shares their journey of healing and transformation with a particular therapist. Their story, filled with personal insights and emotional milestones, paints a vivid picture of what working with that therapist is like. This is the essence of a testimonial's impact. It provides a window into the real-world experiences of others, making the process of therapy more tangible and less abstract.

Hearing about someone's challenges and how they overcame them with the help of a somatic therapist can be incredibly relatable and reassuring. It's one thing to read about a therapist's qualifications and methods but quite another to hear how those methods have tangibly improved someone's life. These personal accounts serve as qualitative evidence of the therapist's ability to effect change, offering a more humanized view of their effectiveness.

Moreover, testimonials can give you a sense of a therapist's unique approach and style – how they interact, communicate, and connect with their clients. This can be particularly important in somatic therapy, where the therapist-client relationship is crucial. Understanding this dynamic through the lens of someone who has experienced it can be immensely helpful in making an informed decision about whether a particular therapist is right for you.

So, to keep it simple, always try to opt for someone with client testimonials and reviews available on their websites or Google pages.

TACKLING BUDGET CONCERNS

If you're interested in somatic therapy but have budget constraints, there are several strategies you can explore to make this form of therapy more accessible:

1. **Sliding Scale Fees:** Many therapists offer sliding scale fees based on income. Feel free to ask a therapist if they provide this option, as it can significantly reduce the cost.

2. **Group Therapy Sessions:** Some therapists offer group sessions, which are often less expensive than individual sessions. Group therapy can provide somatic therapy benefits while offering the support and perspective of peers.

3. **Workshops and Classes:** Look for workshops or classes focusing on somatic practices. These are usually more affordable than ongoing therapy and can be a great introduction to somatic techniques.

4. **Community Health Centers:** Some community health centers or non-profit organizations offer low-cost mental health services, including somatic therapy. They can be an excellent resource for affordable care.

5. **Insurance Coverage:** Check with your insurance provider to see if they cover somatic therapy. Some insurance plans may cover therapy sessions, especially if referred by a physician.

6. **Online Resources:** There are online resources, including videos and articles, which can introduce you to somatic exercises and practices. While this is not a substitute for professional therapy, it can be a good starting point, just like reading this book.

7. **Therapy Schools and Training Programs:** Therapy schools or training programs often offer discounted sessions with therapists-in-training. Experienced professionals supervise these sessions and can be a cost-effective option.

8. **Setting Priorities and Budgeting:** Sometimes, it may be worth revising your budget to prioritize therapy, especially if it's crucial for your well-being. Look at your expenses to see if you can adjust anything to allocate funds for therapy.

9. **Limited Session Plans:** Discuss with a therapist the possibility of a treatment plan with fewer sessions, focusing on key areas. This can help manage costs while still providing therapeutic benefits.

Remember, investing in your mental health is important, and options are available to make therapy more accessible regardless of your budget.

Establishing a Support System: Nurturing a Healing Environment

In the journey of somatic therapy, a good support system plays an integral and transformative role in a patient's recovery. While the individual's engagement in therapy is paramount, the emotional, practical, and motivational backing of friends, family, or a broader community adds a substantial layer of support. This network provides vital emotional sustenance, offering empathy, understanding, and a safe space during times of vulnerability.

It's not just about moral support; often, practical help from loved ones, like assistance with daily tasks or reminders for therapy sessions, can be immensely helpful, especially on challenging days. Additionally, a support system serves as a sounding board and a source of external perspective, helping the patient gauge their progress and stay motivated. It also reduces feelings of isolation, a common challenge in mental health recovery, by reinforcing the idea that the patient is not alone in their journey.

Furthermore, a supportive environment can be instrumental in integrating and reinforcing the practices and techniques learned in somatic therapy into everyday life. Thus, while the patient's efforts in therapy are crucial, the role of a well-rounded support system cannot be overstated in enhancing the overall effectiveness and sustainability of the recovery process.

CREATING A SUPPORT NETWORK

Creating a healthy support system is a proactive process that involves identifying and nurturing relationships based on certain factors. Here's how you can build a supportive network:

1. **Identify Potential Supporters:** Start by identifying people in your life who are understanding, empathetic, and positive. These could be friends, family members, colleagues, or members of a community group.

2. **Communicate Your Needs:** Be open about your needs and what kind of support you seek. This could be emotional support, help with practical tasks, or someone to accompany you to therapy sessions.

3. **Diversify Your Support Network:** Include a mix of people who can offer different types of support. Some might be good listeners, while others might be great at offering practical help or advice.

4. **Participate in Support Groups:** Consider joining support groups related to your specific challenges or therapy goals. These groups can offer understanding, shared experiences, and valuable insights.

5. **Foster Reciprocity:** A healthy support system is reciprocal. Be there for your supporters, offering your help and empathy when they need it.

6. **Set Boundaries:** Establishing healthy boundaries with your support network is important. Clearly communicate your limits and respect others' boundaries as well.

7. **Stay Connected:** Regularly keep in touch with your support network. This could be through phone calls, texts, social media, or in-person meetings.

8. **Appreciate Your Supporters:** Show gratitude to those in your support network. Acknowledging their help and support can strengthen these relationships.

9. **Seek Professional Support if Needed:** Sometimes, you may need more than your friends and family can provide. Don't hesitate to seek support from other mental health professionals.

10. **Cultivate Self-Support:** Alongside external support, work on building internal resources like resilience and self-care practices. This ensures that you have a well-rounded approach to your well-being.

FOSTERING A NURTURING ENVIRONMENT

Creating a nurturing environment and avoiding negative influences is a multi-faceted process that significantly impacts your mental health and well-being. It begins with recognizing toxic elements in your surroundings, which could range from stressful relationships to unhealthy living or working conditions. Understanding what adversely affects you is crucial to initiating change. Setting healthy boundaries is key, especially with individuals or situations that drain your energy or contribute to stress. It involves learning to say no and limiting exposure to negativity.

Simultaneously, it's important to cultivate positive relationships and surround yourself with people who support and uplift you. Your living space also plays a vital role; transforming it into a sanctuary that promotes peace and relaxation can make a significant difference. This might involve decluttering, adding elements that spark joy, or designating areas for relaxation and mindfulness.

In today's digital age, managing media consumption is also

essential. Regular exposure to distressing news or the habit of comparing oneself on social media can adversely affect mental health. Incorporating stress-relieving activities into your daily routine, whether it's engaging in hobbies, exercising, or spending time in nature, can help mitigate the impact of external stressors.

Prioritizing self-care through adequate rest, nutrition, and activities that rejuvenate you is fundamental. A structured daily routine can also provide stability and control, especially in chaotic environments.

Lastly, focusing on personal growth through activities that enhance self-awareness and resilience, like reading, learning new skills, or reflective practices, fortifies your ability to withstand negative environmental influences. While changing certain aspects of your environment may not always be possible, how you respond to these influences can empower you and support your mental health journey.

Setting Healing Intentions: Charting the Course for Recovery

"Healing intentions" refer to the specific goals, aspirations, or desired outcomes an individual sets as part of their therapeutic or personal development journey. These intentions act as guiding principles or focal points in the healing process, whether in therapy, self-care practices, or other forms of personal growth.

Setting healing intentions is also another proactive step in the healing process. It involves reflecting on what you wish to achieve or overcome and what changes you want to see in your life due to therapy or self-healing practices. These intentions can be diverse, ranging from managing specific symptoms, such as reducing anxiety or improving sleep, to broader goals, like achieving a greater sense of peace, improving relationships, or cultivating self-compassion.

In therapy, particularly in approaches like somatic therapy, setting clear healing intentions can help the therapist and the individual focus their efforts more effectively. It creates a roadmap for the therapy process and helps in measuring progress. Healing intentions are not static; they can evolve and change as the individual moves through their healing journey, reflecting new insights, challenges, and growth.

Healing intentions for a person with trauma can differ significantly from those of a person dealing with chronic stress, mainly due to the differing nature and underlying causes of these conditions.

FOR A PERSON WITH TRAUMA:

- Healing intentions often revolve around processing and integrating the traumatic experience. This might include working through feelings of fear, helplessness, and shock that are associated with the trauma.

- A key intention might be to diminish the power of traumatic memories so they no longer trigger intense emotional or physical responses.

- Building a sense of safety in both the body and mind is crucial. Trauma survivors often struggle with feeling safe, so establishing a sense of security is a primary goal.

- Rebuilding trust in themselves and others can be an important intention, as trauma often disrupts trust.

- Reconnecting with the body is also a common intention, as trauma can lead to disassociation or disconnection from bodily sensations.

FOR A PERSON WITH CHRONIC STRESS:

- Healing intentions might focus more on developing effective stress management skills and strategies to cope with daily pressures.

- A major intention could be to establish a balanced lifestyle that includes time for relaxation and self-care to mitigate the effects of stress.

- Identifying and modifying unhelpful thought patterns that contribute to stress is often a key goal.

- Improving physical health through exercise, nutrition, and sleep, which chronic stress can adversely affect, might also be a primary intention.

- Building resilience to handle future stressors and challenges is typically a central focus.

While there is some overlap in the intentions for both conditions — such as developing self-awareness and emotional regulation skills — the specific goals and approaches in therapy will vary based on the individual's unique experiences and needs. For trauma, the focus is often on healing deep-seated emotional wounds and restoring a sense of safety. In contrast, for chronic stress, it's more about developing ongoing strategies to manage everyday stressors and improve overall well-being.

Chapter Summary

KEY TAKEAWAYS

1. **Finding a Somatic Therapist:** When looking for a somatic therapist, consider factors like qualifications, experience, therapeutic approach, and personal compatibility. Assessing the therapist's understanding of your specific needs is crucial.

2. **Red Flags in a Therapist:** Be aware of red flags like lack of boundaries, disregard for client comfort and unrealistic promises. A good therapist should maintain professionalism and prioritize your well-being.

3. **The Power of Testimonials:** Testimonials can provide relatable and personal insights into a therapist's effectiveness and can be a valuable resource in selecting the right therapist.

4. **Budget-Friendly Options:** If budget is a concern, explore sliding scale fees, group therapy sessions, community health centers, and online resources for more affordable options.

5. **Importance of a Support System:** A supportive network of friends, family, or peer groups enhances the effectiveness of somatic therapy, providing emotional and practical support throughout the healing journey.

6. **Creating a Healthy Environment:** Cultivating a nurturing environment and avoiding negative influences are key to mental health. This includes setting boundaries, fostering positive relationships, and engaging in self-care practices.

7. **Setting Healing Intentions:** Clear healing intentions are important in somatic therapy. For trauma survivors, intentions often focus on processing the trauma and rebuilding safety, while for chronic stress, they might center on stress management and lifestyle balance.

8. **Healing Intentions for Trauma vs. Chronic Stress:** Healing intentions differ for trauma and chronic stress, focusing on safety and processing trauma in the former and stress management and lifestyle balance in the latter.

Try the next chapter to understand the kinds of tools and techniques a therapist will employ during your sessions.

My Note

Chapter 7

Tools and Techniques for Healing

In this enlightening chapter, we delve into the heart of somatic therapy, exploring the various tools and techniques that form the essence of this transformative practice. With its unique focus on the interplay between body and mind, somatic therapy employs a diverse array of methods to facilitate healing and personal growth. This chapter aims to illuminate these methods, providing a deeper understanding of how they work and their benefits in the therapeutic process.

We will explore breathwork's calming and centering power, a fundamental aspect of somatic therapy that helps regulate the body's stress response and enhance emotional awareness. The chapter will also introduce you to somatic experiencing, a technique developed to release and resolve the physical manifestations of trauma stored in the body.

Additionally, we will examine the role of muscle relaxation techniques, which are crucial in addressing the physical symptoms of stress and trauma. These techniques aid in releasing muscle tension and contribute to overall emotional and mental relaxation.

Other tools and techniques, such as mindful movement, guided imagery, and grounding exercises, will be discussed to provide a comprehensive overview of the somatic therapy toolbox. Each of these techniques offers a unique pathway to connect with and understand the body's language, fostering healing from within.

This chapter is designed to be both informative and practical, offering insights into how these tools and techniques can be applied in therapy sessions and everyday life. Whether you are a therapy practitioner, someone on their healing journey, or simply seeking a deeper understanding of somatic therapy, this chapter will guide you through the rich and varied landscape of somatic practices.

Breathwork: Harnessing the Power of Breath for Healing

Breathing is powerful, yet we fail to harness its full potential. Why is that? Despite its fundamental role in our well-being, it is often overlooked in the context of recovery and healing. This oversight occurs partly because breathing is an automatic process; we do it without conscious thought, making it easy to underestimate its significance. However, how we breathe holds many answers to recovery, especially in somatic therapy.

Scientifically, breathing is the physiological process of inhaling oxygen and exhaling carbon dioxide, essential for life. It's a vital function that sustains the body's various systems, but it also profoundly impacts our mental and emotional states, making it crucial for relaxation practices.

The importance of breathing in relaxation lies in its direct influence on the autonomic nervous system, which regulates involuntary body functions, including heart rate and digestion. This system has two main components: the sympathetic nervous system (SNS), which triggers the 'fight or flight' response during stress, and the parasympathetic nervous system (PNS), which activates the 'rest and digest' state, promoting relaxation and healing.

Our breathing patterns change when we're stressed, anxious, or traumatized. These situations often trigger shallow, rapid breaths that heighten our body's stress response. Such a breathing pattern can perpetuate feelings of anxiety and tension. Conversely, deep and controlled breathing can activate the body's relaxation response. It sends a signal to the brain to calm down and relax, which slows the heart rate and lowers blood pressure, helping to reduce stress.

How is all of that relevant to you? In somatic therapy, focused breathing exercises are used to connect with the body and regulate emotional states. By consciously changing breathing patterns, individuals like yourself can gain control over their physiological and psychological responses to stress. This control is particularly powerful in trauma recovery, where regulating the nervous system is a key component of healing.

Furthermore, breathwork can be a gateway to increased body awareness. It encourages individuals to tune into their physical sensations, fostering mindfulness and presence. This heightened awareness can lead to insights into how emotions are experienced in the body, contributing to deeper emotional processing and healing.

In summary, breathing is a fundamental physical process and a bridge to mental and emotional well-being. Its ability to influence the autonomic nervous system and foster mindfulness makes it a key component in relaxation practices. It offers an accessible and effective way to manage stress and promote a sense of calm.

EFFECTS OF THE BODY'S STRESS RESPONSE ON BREATHING

When a person is traumatized or stressed, several changes in their breathing patterns can occur, reflecting the body's natural response to perceived threats or distress. These abnormal patterns are often part of the body's instinctive fight-or-flight response, regulated by the sympathetic nervous system. Common changes in breathing patterns include:

1. **Shallow Breathing:** Under stress or trauma, breathing becomes shallow and restricted. Instead of deep, diaphragmatic breaths, the breaths are typically short and rapid, occurring in the upper chest. This type of breathing can limit oxygen intake and exacerbate feelings of anxiety or agitation.

2. **Rapid Breathing:** Also known as hyperventilation, rapid breathing is common during acute stress or anxiety. This can lead to decreased carbon dioxide levels in the blood, which may cause symptoms like dizziness, light-headedness, or a feeling of breathlessness.

3. **Irregular Breathing:** Stress and trauma can disrupt the natural breathing rhythm, leading to irregular or erratic breathing patterns. This might involve alternating between fast and slow breaths or unpredictable pauses in breathing.

4. **Holding the Breath:** Some individuals unconsciously hold their breath or have very shallow breaths when they are in a state of heightened stress or recalling a traumatic event. This is often a subconscious effort to brace against fear or pain.

5. **Chest Tightness:** Stress and anxiety can lead to a sensation of tightness in the chest, which can further impact breathing patterns, making it difficult to take deep, full breaths.

These abnormal breathing patterns can contribute to a cycle of increased physical tension and psychological distress. You can learn to recognize and address these patterns through breathwork and relaxation techniques, managing stress and trauma responses more effectively.

BREATHWORK TECHNIQUES USED FOR SOMATIC THERAPY

You inhale and exhale; how much simpler can it get? Well, turns out that there's a lot you can do by implementing minute changes in your breath patterns. Breathwork techniques employed during somatic therapy are diverse and aim to utilize the breath to facilitate emotional and physical healing. These techniques are based on the principle that by changing our breathing patterns, we can influence our mental and emotional states. Here are some common breathwork techniques you can expect to be used during somatic therapy:

1. **Diaphragmatic Breathing:** This technique encourages deep breaths that fully engage the diaphragm, a large muscle located at the base of the lungs. Practitioners guide clients to focus on expanding their abdomen rather than their chest as they inhale, which promotes deeper breathing and activates the parasympathetic nervous system, the body's relaxation response. This kind of breathing is especially beneficial for reducing the physiological symptoms of stress and anxiety.

2. **Rhythmic Breathing:** This involves breathing in a consistent, rhythmic pattern, often with equal time allocated to inhaling, holding the breath, and exhaling. This technique can help regulate the body's stress response by focusing on maintaining a steady rhythm, bringing about a sense of calm and balance. It's particularly useful for individuals who experience irregular breathing patterns due to anxiety or panic attacks.

3. **Breath Awareness:** In this simple yet powerful practice, the focus is on observing the natural flow of breath without trying to alter it. It enhances mindfulness and helps individuals become more attuned to their emotional and physical state. This technique is often used as a grounding exercise, helping clients to anchor themselves in the present moment and disengage from distressing thoughts or emotions.

4. **4-7-8 Breathing:** This technique, developed by Dr. Andrew Weil, involves inhaling for four seconds, holding the breath for seven seconds, and exhaling for eight seconds. It's designed to act as a natural tranquilizer for the nervous system, slowing down the heart rate and promoting deep relaxation. It's particularly effective in managing stress and anxiety and helping with insomnia.

5. **Alternate Nostril Breathing (Nadi Shodhana):** Originating from yoga traditions, this technique involves using the thumb and finger to alternately close each nostril while breathing. Practice is believed to balance the brain's two hemispheres, resulting in physical, mental, and emotional well-being. It's often used to enhance concentration, relieve stress, and support overall mental balance.

6. **Sighing and Yawning:** Deliberate sighing and yawning can be used to reset the breathing pattern and release tension. A deep sigh, often a natural response to fatigue or stress, can quickly relieve anxiety or stress. Similarly, yawning can help relax the facial muscles and reduce stress.

7. **Guided Imagery and Breath:** This combines controlled breathing with guided imagery, where clients are led through calming visualizations or narratives. This combination can deepen the relaxation response, as the mental imagery can amplify the calming effects of the breathwork.

8. **Breathing into Sensations:** Practitioners guide clients to direct their breath to areas of the body where they experience tension or discomfort. This technique is based on the principle that focused breathing can help release physical tension and associated emotional pain.

Each technique offers unique benefits and can be tailored to the individual's needs and preferences in a therapeutic setting. They are tools not only for immediate stress relief but also for long-term emotional regulation and self-awareness. The next time you feel anxious for no reason, why don't you try one of the above and see if it works? (I guarantee you, it will!)

Somatic Experiencing: Engaging the Body's Wisdom

THE BODY'S WISDOM

It sounds like an ethereal and ancient idea, but what does it mean in the modern context? The concept of the "body's wisdom" embodies the understanding that our bodies possess an innate knowledge and insight about our emotional and physical well-being, often surpassing the immediate awareness of our conscious minds. This idea, central to holistic healing practices like somatic therapy, suggests that our bodies respond intuitively to experiences and emotions, often before our conscious mind fully processes them.

For instance, physical sensations such as a 'gut feeling' can intuitively guide decision-making. Moreover, our bodies can store memories of emotional and traumatic events, evidenced by physical responses or tension linked to past experiences, which might not be active in our conscious memory. This concept also highlights the body's natural ability to heal and regulate itself, indicating that tuning into these bodily signals can lead to practices that foster healing and overall well-being. It underscores the deep interconnection between mind and body, where emotional and mental states manifest physically, and addressing physical states can, in turn, impact emotional health.

In therapeutic contexts, recognizing and understanding the body's wisdom can be crucial in guiding the healing process, helping to uncover underlying issues and inform effective therapeutic approaches. Embracing the body's wisdom encourages a respectful and attentive relationship with our bodies, viewing them not just as systems with symptoms to be treated but as integral parts of our being that offer valuable insights into our health and life experiences. With Somatic Experiencing, tapping into this wisdom becomes possible.

HOW SOMATIC EXPERIENCING WAS DISCOVERED

Somatic Experiencing (SE) is a therapeutic approach developed by Dr. Peter Levine aimed at relieving the symptoms of mental and physical trauma-related health problems. Dr. Peter Levine's development of Somatic Experiencing (SE) is a fascinating story that combines observations from nature, insights from medical and psychological research, and practical therapeutic applications.

Dr. Levine's journey began in the 1970s when he was studying stress in animals and humans. He was particularly intrigued by how animals in the wild, despite regularly facing life-threatening dangers, rarely showed signs of trauma. This observation led him to explore how animals seemingly prevent traumatic reactions. He noted that after a threatening event, animals engage in instinctive movements such as shaking or running, which appeared to help them 'discharge' and recover from the high-energy state of arousal caused by the threat.

Dr. Levine applied these observations to the human experience of trauma. He theorized that humans have a natural capacity to regulate and recover from stress and trauma like animals. However, cultural and behavioral factors often inhibit these instinctual responses, leading to the energy associated with trauma becoming 'stuck' in the body. He drew upon his background in medical biophysics and psychology and his studies in stress, neuroscience, psychophysiology, and indigenous healing practices to develop a framework that would help release this trapped energy.

Somatic Experiencing was developed as a body-focused therapeutic approach to trauma. It emphasizes the body's role in trauma and recovery, focusing on the client's bodily sensations and reactions as keys to unlocking and healing trauma. Dr. Levine introduced the concepts of 'titration' and 'pendulation' in the therapy process. Titration involves slowly exposing the client to traumatic memories to avoid re-traumatization. Pendulation refers to guiding the client in oscillating between states of trauma activation and states of safety or relief, gradually increasing their capacity to manage and process traumatic reactions.

Over the years, Dr. Levine refined his approach through clinical work and research. He authored several books, including his seminal work, "Waking the Tiger: Healing Trauma," which brought Somatic Experiencing to a wider audience. Today, SE is recognized as an effective approach to treating trauma and is practiced by therapists worldwide.

SOMATIC EXPERIENCING: THE PROCESS

The process of somatic experiencing (SE) is rooted in the understanding that trauma symptoms are the effects of dysregulation in the autonomic nervous system (ANS) and that the body holds key information about these traumatic experiences. Here's a detailed look at the SE process:

1. Establishing Safety and Resources:

- The first step in SE is creating a safe therapeutic environment. It's crucial for clients to feel secure and supported.

- Clients are also helped to identify resources that help them feel calm and grounded, such as certain memories, images, sensations, or physical objects.

2. Building Awareness of Bodily Sensations:

- SE emphasizes the importance of bodily awareness. Clients are guided to notice bodily sensations, like tension or temperature changes, which can indicate trapped traumatic energy.

- The therapist helps the client to focus on these sensations without becoming overwhelmed, fostering a sense of curiosity and exploration.

3. Titration and Pendulation:

- Titration involves breaking down the traumatic experience into small, manageable parts to avoid re-traumatization.

- Pendulation is moving the client's attention between traumatic memories (activation) and resources or neutral places (deactivation). This helps the client learn that they can move out of a traumatic response and into a state of safety.

4. Discharging Traumatic Energy:

- SE posits that trauma disrupts the body's ability to release high-energy responses associated with fight, flight, or freeze reactions.

- The therapist guides the client to slowly release this trapped energy, often through physical movements, shaking, or other natural responses.

5. Integration:

- After discharging energy, the therapist assists the client in integrating these experiences. Integration means allowing the body and mind to assimilate and process the released emotions and sensations.

- This step is crucial for restoring balance to the ANS and helping the client realize they have moved past the traumatic event.

6. Expansion of Tolerance:

- Throughout the process, SE expands the client's tolerance for difficult bodily sensations and emotions. This is done slowly and carefully to ensure the client is not re-traumatized.

- The goal is to increase the client's capacity to handle stress and emotional challenges without becoming dysregulated.

7. Encouraging Self-Regulation:

- A key outcome of SE is the development of greater self-regulation. Clients learn techniques to manage their own emotional and physiological states.

- The therapist empowers the client to use these skills outside therapy, promoting long-term resilience and well-being.

8. Closure and Reconnection:

- The final phase of SE involves creating a sense of closure from the trauma and reconnecting the client to their present life.

- Clients are encouraged to engage in life with a renewed sense of safety, empowerment, and presence.

Somatic Experiencing is a gradual, respectful process that honors the client's pace and comfort level. To give you the pocket-sized explanation, you will slowly learn to conquer the trauma by reliving and resetting yourself through your triggers, training your body and mind to intentionally cope with those experiences, and consequently overcome them.

Body Scan and Progressive Muscle Relaxation Techniques

Body scan and muscle relaxation techniques are integral components of somatic therapy, helping individuals connect with their bodies, identify areas of tension or trauma, and promote relaxation and healing.

BODY SCAN TECHNIQUE

The body scan is a mindfulness exercise that involves mentally scanning oneself from head to toe. During this scan, individuals are guided to pay attention to different parts of their body, noticing any sensations, tensions, or discomfort.

The process encourages awareness of the body without judgment. As individuals move their focus through each area, they learn to recognize how stress, trauma, or emotional issues manifest physically.

By bringing awareness to these areas, the body scan can help identify and release stored tension and trauma. It's often used as a starting point in Somatic Therapy to heighten body awareness and prepare for deeper therapeutic work.

The body scan can be particularly effective in reducing symptoms of stress and anxiety, improving sleep, and enhancing overall mindfulness and presence.

MUSCLE RELAXATION TECHNIQUES

Muscle relaxation techniques in Somatic Therapy often involve consciously tensing and relaxing different muscle groups. This is known as Progressive Muscle Relaxation (PMR).

PMR helps individuals become more aware of physical sensations associated with tension and relaxation. PMR can significantly reduce overall bodily tension by systematically working through different muscle groups.

These techniques are not only used to alleviate physical tension but also to lower mental and emotional stress. There's a close connection between muscular tension and psychological states; relaxing the muscles can thus lead to a calmer mind.

Muscle relaxation techniques can also include gentle stretching, movement exercises, or specific postures that release tension and improve physical alignment and comfort.

Both body scanning and muscle relaxation techniques are powerful tools in somatic therapy. They help bridge the gap between the physical and emotional, offering pathways to understand and heal the impacts of stress and trauma on the body.

Chapter Summary

In conclusion, this chapter delved into somatic therapy's essential tools and techniques, highlighting how this approach harnesses the body's innate wisdom for healing and recovery.

We explored the profound role of breathwork in managing stress and trauma, utilizing various breathing techniques to regulate the autonomic nervous system and promote relaxation.

We then examined Somatic Experiencing (SE), developed by Dr. Peter Levine, which focuses on releasing traumatic energy stored in the body through a process that includes building awareness, titration, pendulation, and the gradual discharge of this energy.

Additionally, we discussed the therapeutic benefits of body scans and muscle relaxation techniques. The body scan technique, a form of mindful observation, helps identify and release tension and trauma held in the body. Progressive Muscle Relaxation (PMR) and other muscle relaxation methods actively reduce physical tension, which can alleviate mental and emotional stress.

Each of these techniques is something you can expect to encounter when you first start your somatic therapy sessions.

My Note

Chapter 8

Navigating Emotional Release

Navigating your emotions and learning to regulate them can be a complex and often challenging process, yet it is a critical aspect of the healing journey. Emotional release is an integral part of recovering from trauma, managing stress, and achieving personal growth. This chapter aims to provide a comprehensive understanding of how to effectively navigate this process, focusing on understanding triggers, processing emotions, and cultivating a self-compassionate approach.

We begin by exploring the concept of 'triggers' - external events or internal thoughts that can evoke intense emotional responses, often linked to past trauma or stressful experiences. Understanding these triggers is the first step in managing emotional responses and preventing overwhelming feelings. This section will guide you through identifying your personal triggers and developing strategies to cope with them effectively.

Next, we delve into the heart of emotional processing. This involves learning how to safely experience and express emotions rather than avoiding or suppressing them. We will discuss techniques and tools that facilitate this process, emphasizing the importance of acknowledging and working through emotions to achieve true healing.

Lastly, the chapter highlights the importance of cultivating a self-compassionate approach throughout this journey. Self-compassion is a powerful tool in healing, offering kindness and understanding to oneself during moments of emotional difficulty. We will explore how to develop and maintain a compassionate attitude towards oneself, which can transform the experience of emotional release from struggle to gentle, nurturing growth.

Let's see how you can master your emotions.

Understanding Emotional Triggers: Unraveling Emotional Patterns

EMOTIONS VS. THOUGHTS

You say, "I feel like..." in a different context than "I think..." Emotions and thoughts are distinct yet interconnected aspects of our psychological experience, and both play significant roles in therapy.

Emotions are complex psychological and physiological responses to internal or external events. They are often experienced physically in the body and can manifest as sensations like a racing heart (anxiety), a heavy chest (sadness), or a flushed face (anger). Emotions are often immediate and can be triggered by thoughts or external stimuli. They are not inherently rational and can vary greatly in intensity and duration.

Conversely, thoughts are mental processes where we interpret, analyze, and make sense of the world around us. Thoughts are the cognitive interpretations or narratives we create about our experiences. They can be conscious or unconscious and are influenced by our beliefs, past experiences, and perceptions. Thoughts can shape our emotions, but emotional states can also influence them.

In the context of therapy, both emotions and thoughts are crucial, but their importance may vary depending on the therapeutic approach and the individual's needs.

In cognitive-based therapies, such as Cognitive Behavioral Therapy (CBT), thoughts are often given greater weight initially. The focus is on identifying and changing maladaptive or irrational thoughts, which are seen as leading to negative emotions and behaviors.

In contrast, emotion-focused therapies, like Gestalt Therapy or Somatic Experiencing, place more emphasis on emotions. These approaches work on the premise that understanding and processing emotions are key to resolving psychological issues.

However, most modern therapeutic approaches recognize the interplay between thoughts and emotions. They understand that addressing one without the other might not provide a comprehensive solution. For instance, merely changing a thought pattern without addressing the underlying emotional response may lead to incomplete healing.

While thoughts and emotions serve different functions, they are deeply interconnected. Effective therapy often involves understanding and working with both, tailored to the individual's needs and the nature of their challenges.

EMOTIONAL TRIGGERS

"Oh, that was so triggering!" is a common response from someone feeling agitated, but triggers are not limited to anger. In psychological terms, an emotional trigger refers to a stimulus — such as sight, sound, smell, or memory — that provokes a strong emotional reaction, often linked to a past experience or trauma. These triggers activate certain neural pathways in the brain, particularly in the amygdala, which is involved in emotional processing. When triggered, the amygdala sets off a chain of biochemical responses in the body, preparing it for a 'fight or flight' response. This reaction can be disproportionate to the trigger itself, but it is the brain's way of protecting the individual from perceived danger based on past experiences.

Triggers can lead to a range of emotions, including anxiety, sadness, anger, or panic, and can often cause distress or disruption in an individual's life. Understanding and identifying one's emotional triggers is critical in therapeutic contexts. It involves aspects of cognitive psychology, which focuses on recognizing and altering thought patterns, and behavioral psychology, which looks at the relationship between stimuli and reactions.

By learning to identify and manage these triggers, individuals can develop better coping strategies and reduce their impact, which is a key aspect of trauma-informed therapy and emotional regulation techniques. Clarifying emotional triggers is crucial in the journey towards emotional healing and resilience.

A DISPLAY OF GETTING EMOTIONALLY TRIGGERED

Sarah is a young professional in her late twenties. Sarah had a generally happy life but found herself inexplicably overwhelmed by anxiety in certain situations. It all started making sense when she began therapy and learned about emotional triggers.

One day, Sarah was walking through the park on her way to work, a route she took every day. This morning, she heard a car backfire loudly, a sound that instantly made her heart race, her palms sweat, and filled her with an inexplicable sense of dread. Confused and unsettled by her reaction, she arrived at work feeling out of sorts.

In her therapy session, Sarah discussed the incident. Her therapist explained that the loud noise had likely triggered this response. They delved deeper, exploring Sarah's past experiences, and discovered that she had been in a minor car accident as a teenager. Although Sarah had thought she had moved past the accident, her body and subconscious mind still remembered the trauma associated with that loud, sudden noise.

Understanding this, Sarah's therapist worked with her to recognize and manage these triggers. They used a combination of therapeutic modules to help Sarah reframe her thoughts around sudden loud noises and practiced mindfulness exercises to reduce her physiological response.

Over time, Sarah learned to identify other triggers and developed strategies to cope with them. She began to understand how certain sights, sounds, and even smells could unconsciously remind her of past events, causing her emotional and physical distress.

Learning how to recognize and manage emotional triggers was transformative for Sarah. It not only helped her handle her anxiety but also gave her deeper insights into how her past experiences were shaping her present reactions. With this understanding, Sarah felt more in control and equipped to face situations that had previously caused her distress, leading her towards healing and emotional resilience.

EMOTIONAL PATTERNS

Emotional patterns refer to repetitive, habitual emotional responses or reactions that a person experiences in various situations. These patterns are often deeply ingrained and can be rooted in past experiences, beliefs, or learned behavior. They play a significant role in how individuals perceive and interact with the world around them. Here's a closer look at emotional patterns:

1. **Formation:** Emotional patterns often develop over time, starting in childhood. Early experiences, family dynamics, cultural background, and significant life events can shape them. For example, a person who frequently experienced criticism in childhood might develop a pattern of feeling anxious or defensive in situations where they perceive potential judgment or failure.

2. Triggering: These patterns can be triggered by specific situations, people, or even internal thoughts that resonate with past experiences. When triggered, the individual might automatically respond with a familiar emotional reaction, even if it's not appropriate or helpful in the current context.

3. Consistency: Emotional patterns tend to be consistent over time and can become a default way of responding emotionally. This can lead to predictable emotional responses in certain scenarios, regardless of the present reality or differing circumstances.

4. Impact: These patterns can significantly influence behavior, decision-making, relationships, and overall mental health. They might lead to recurrent issues, such as conflict in relationships, chronic stress, or avoidance of certain situations.

5. Change and Awareness: Recognizing and changing emotional patterns can be a focus in therapy. This process involves becoming aware of these patterns, understanding their origins, and learning new, healthier ways to respond emotionally. Techniques like mindfulness, cognitive-behavioral strategies, and emotional processing can be used to alter these patterns.

There is a greater interplay between emotional patterns and triggers that cause a cascade of unpleasant reactions within a person, which we'll establish next.

THE LINK BETWEEN PATTERNS AND TRIGGERS

Emotional patterns are the habitual ways a person responds emotionally to certain stimuli or situations. Conversely, triggers are specific stimuli — events, words, people, or even thoughts — that activate these emotional patterns.

When a trigger is encountered, it sets off a chain reaction that taps into an established emotional pattern. For example, if someone has an emotional pattern of feeling inadequate (perhaps developed through early experiences of criticism), encountering a situation that remotely hints at criticism or judgment (the trigger) can instantly evoke feelings of inadequacy or defensiveness, regardless of the current reality of the situation.

This connection can be understood in terms of neural pathways in the brain. Emotional patterns are like well-trodden paths in the brain formed through repeated activation over time. When a trigger is experienced, it quickly travels down this familiar path, leading to a habitual emotional response. This process often occurs subconsciously, making individuals react in predictable ways without fully understanding why.

The relationship between emotional patterns and triggers is crucial in therapeutic contexts. Therapy often involves identifying and understanding one's triggers, recognizing the underlying emotional patterns, and then working to alter these patterns to create healthier emotional responses. By doing so, individuals can learn to respond to triggers more balanced and less reactive, leading to improved emotional regulation and well-being.

Processing and Releasing Stored Emotions: Safe and Effective Practices

EMOTIONAL PROCESSING

Emotional processing is a therapeutic concept that refers to how individuals experience, understand, and work through their emotions. It involves both the recognition of emotions and the ability to manage and integrate them into one's experience. Here's an overview of emotional processing:

1. Recognition and Acknowledgment: Emotional processing begins with recognizing and acknowledging one's emotions. This involves becoming aware of how you feel in response to certain events, thoughts, or situations, and accepting these emotions as valid, regardless of their nature.

2. **Understanding:** The next step is understanding why you feel a certain way. This may involve exploring the roots of these emotions, which could be linked to past experiences, underlying beliefs, or current stressors. Understanding the 'why' behind emotions is key to processing them effectively.

3. **Expression:** Healthy emotional processing involves expressing emotions in appropriate ways. This could be through talking about them, writing, engaging in creative activities, or even physical activities like exercise. Expression is a crucial part of processing as it allows for externalizing internal emotional states.

4. **Regulation:** Emotional regulation is the ability to manage and modulate emotional responses in a way that is appropriate to the situation. This includes techniques like deep breathing, mindfulness, and cognitive reframing to help control overwhelming emotions.

5. **Integration:** Emotional processing involves integrating these emotions into one's larger experience. This means accepting and making peace with emotions, learning from them, and allowing them to inform but not control your future reactions and decisions.

Effective emotional processing is not about eliminating negative emotions but rather about developing a healthy relationship with all emotions. It's a vital skill that allows individuals to navigate their emotional landscape with greater ease and resilience, leading to improved mental health and quality of life. Therapy often focuses on enhancing emotional processing skills, especially for individuals who struggle with emotional regulation or have experienced trauma.

EMOTIONAL RELEASE

Emotional release in the context of somatic therapy is a process where deep-seated, often unconscious emotions are brought to the surface and expressed, leading to a sense of relief and healing. In somatic therapy, emotional release is often a pivotal moment in the healing process. It can happen when clients become deeply aware of their bodily sensations during therapy. As the therapist guides the client to focus on areas of tension or discomfort in the body, these sensations can trigger the release of emotions that have been stored or repressed. This release can manifest in various forms, such as crying, trembling, laughing, or even vocal expressions.

The process is not about forcing emotions out but rather allowing them to emerge naturally. Somatic therapists create a safe and supportive space for this release, ensuring clients feel secure and grounded. They use techniques like breathwork, gentle movement, or guided imagery to help facilitate this process.

Emotional release in somatic therapy is considered to be both cathartic and restorative. It's cathartic in the sense that it provides a release of emotional energy that has been pent up, often for years. This release can lead to a significant reduction in physical and emotional symptoms associated with that repressed energy, such as chronic tension, anxiety, or mood disturbances. It's restorative because it allows for a reintegration of the emotional experience, enabling the client to process and healthily make sense of these emotions.

This process is integral to the philosophy of somatic therapy, which sees the mind and body as interconnected and believes that healing the mind involves addressing the body as well. Emotional release is thus a key step in achieving a harmonious balance between mind and body, leading to holistic healing and well-being.

SOMATIC METHODS USED FOR PROCESSING AND RELEASING EMOTIONS

In somatic therapy, various methods help clients process and safely release stored emotions. These methods focus on connecting the body and mind, using bodily awareness and experiences as gateways to emotional healing. Here's an overview of some key techniques:

1. **Mindful Body Awareness:** This involves guiding clients to focus on their bodily sensations in the present moment. By becoming aware of where and how emotions are experienced in the body,

clients can start to recognize and process these emotions. For instance, shoulder tension might be linked to stress or holding back emotions.

2. **Breathwork:** Breathing techniques regulate the nervous system and facilitate emotional release. Deep, rhythmic breathing can help calm the body and create a safe space for emotions to surface and be expressed.

3. **Movement and Dance:** Movement therapies, including dance, can help clients physically express and release emotions. Through movement, clients can explore and express feelings that might be difficult to articulate verbally.

4. **Guided Imagery and Visualization:** These techniques involve guiding clients through mental images or scenarios that can help unlock and process emotions. For example, visualizing a safe place can help in accessing and releasing fear or anxiety.

5. **Physical Touch and Manipulation:** In some forms of somatic therapy, gentle touch or physical manipulation (like massage or pressure on certain body parts) can release tension and facilitate emotional release. This is always done with the client's consent and comfort in mind.

6. **Pendulation:** A technique specific to Somatic Experiencing, pendulation involves oscillating the client's attention between sensations associated with trauma (activation) and sensations of safety or neutrality (deactivation). This helps in gradually reducing the intensity of traumatic responses.

7. **Titration:** This method involves slowly and carefully exposing the client to emotional content, ensuring they do not become overwhelmed. It's about breaking down the emotional experience into manageable parts.

8. **Grounding Exercises:** These techniques help clients stay connected to the present moment and feel more rooted in their bodies, counterbalancing the sometimes-intense emotions that can arise during therapy.

9. **Expressive Arts Therapy:** Incorporating arts such as drawing, painting, or writing can provide alternative outlets for expressing and processing emotions.

10. **Integration Techniques:** Post-emotional release, clients are assisted in integrating their experiences through reflection, discussion, and cognitive processing.

These methods are tailored to each individual's needs and experiences. Somatic therapists are trained to guide clients through these techniques in a safe, respectful, and supportive way, ensuring that emotional release is part of a holistic healing process.

Self-Compassion in Healing: Cultivating a Gentle Approach

The significance of self-compassion in mental health recovery cannot be overstated. It is vital to healing and growth, offering a kind, nurturing approach to oneself during challenging times. Self-compassion involves treating oneself with the same kindness, concern, and support one would offer to a good friend.

In the context of mental health recovery, self-compassion plays several key roles:

1. **Reducing Self-Criticism:** Individuals struggling with mental health issues often experience heightened levels of self-criticism and negative self-talk. Self-compassion helps counteract these harmful patterns by encouraging a more understanding and forgiving attitude towards oneself.

2. **Managing Difficult Emotions:** Self-compassion provides a framework for dealing with difficult emotions gently and acceptingly. Instead of suppressing or being overwhelmed by such emotions, self-compassion allows individuals to acknowledge and sit with their feelings, understanding that experiencing pain and suffering is part of being human.

3. **Enhancing Resilience:** Self-compassionate individuals tend to be more resilient in the face of stress and adversity. By being kind and supportive to themselves, they are better equipped to bounce back from difficult situations.

4. **Promoting Positive Self-Relationship:** Developing self-compassion leads to a healthier, more positive relationship with oneself. This improved self-relationship is crucial for mental health recovery, as it fosters self-acceptance and personal growth.

5. **Reducing Shame and Stigma:** Self-compassion can help in breaking down feelings of shame and stigma associated with mental health issues. Recognizing that one is not alone in their struggle allows for a more open and accepting approach to recovery.

6. **Encouraging Help-Seeking Behavior:** A self-compassionate attitude can make it easier for individuals to seek help and support. Understanding that seeking help is a sign of strength and self-care, not weakness, can motivate individuals to engage in therapeutic processes more willingly.

7. **Supporting Long-Term Well-Being:** Self-compassion is not just beneficial during times of crisis; it's a sustainable practice that supports long-term mental health and well-being. It encourages an ongoing, nurturing relationship with oneself that can withstand life's ups and downs.

Incorporating self-compassion into mental health recovery is transformative. It shifts the focus from self-judgment and criticism to understanding and acceptance, paving the way for healing and a more fulfilling life.

If you're feeling like you're struggling against yourself, I want to offer you some words of kindness and encouragement. First and foremost, know that you are not alone in this. Many of us face internal battles, and it's okay to feel overwhelmed at times. Your feelings are valid, and it's important to acknowledge them.

Remember, being hard on yourself doesn't make the journey any easier. Instead, treat yourself with the same compassion and understanding you would offer a good friend. You deserve that same patience and kindness, especially from yourself.

It's okay to take a step back and breathe. Give yourself permission to rest, feel, and be in the moment without judgment. Every step you take, no matter how small, is progress. Healing and growth take time, so be gentle with yourself along the way.

You have a reservoir of strength within you, even if it doesn't feel like it right now. You are capable and resilient. Allow yourself to lean on this strength and remember that seeking help is a courageous and positive step towards healing.

Celebrate your successes, no matter how small they seem. Every effort you make in understanding and caring for yourself is significant. You're doing your best with where you are right now, and that is enough.

Cultivate a gentle approach towards yourself. This journey is not about perfection but about learning, growing, and finding balance. You are worthy of love and care — start by giving it to yourself. You are more than your struggles; with time and self-compassion, you will find your way to a brighter, kinder place.

As you go through each chapter, I hope that you're one step closer to the solace you're looking for. One practical way to attain this is through mindfulness and meditation, which we'll look at next

My Note

Chapter 9

Integrating Mindfulness and Meditation

Integrating mindfulness and meditation into somatic practices marks a critical intersection, enriching the therapeutic process with depth and introspection. This chapter aims to illuminate how these ancient practices bolster modern therapeutic approaches, contributing significantly to healing and personal growth.

We begin by delving into the essence of mindfulness — a practice of present-moment awareness, non-judgmental observation, and acceptance. In the context of somatic therapy, mindfulness becomes a powerful tool, enabling individuals to tune into their bodily sensations and emotions with greater clarity and understanding. We'll explore how mindfulness enhances body awareness, a cornerstone of somatic therapy, and aids in recognizing and processing deeply rooted emotional and physical experiences.

Next, we turn to meditation, a practice often intertwined with mindfulness yet possessing its unique qualities. Meditation, in its various forms, offers a pathway to inner stillness and heightened awareness. We will examine its role in regulating the autonomic nervous system, calming the mind, and creating a therapeutic space for deep healing.

Furthermore, this chapter will explore how mindfulness and meditation can transform the way individuals respond to stress, trauma, and emotional pain. By fostering balance and equanimity, these practices empower individuals to approach their recovery journey with greater resilience and self-compassion.

Whether you are new to these practices or looking to deepen your existing knowledge, this chapter offers valuable insights into integrating mindfulness and meditation into your therapeutic journey.

Mindfulness Practices: Enhancing Body Awareness

Mindfulness is a mental practice that involves maintaining a moment-by-moment awareness of our thoughts, feelings, bodily sensations, and the surrounding environment. It's characterized by acceptance, meaning that attention is paid to thoughts and feelings without judging them—without believing, for instance, that there's a "right" or "wrong" way to think or feel in a given moment.

At its core, mindfulness is about being fully present in the moment and engaged with whatever we're doing, free from distraction or judgment, and aware of our thoughts and feelings without getting caught up in them. This can be achieved through various practices, including meditation, but can also be incorporated into everyday life by bringing intentional attention and awareness to our daily activities and experiences.

The practice of mindfulness has its roots in Buddhist meditation, but it has been secularized and popularized in the West largely through the work of people like Jon Kabat-Zinn. Kabat-Zinn's Mindfulness-Based Stress Reduction (MBSR) program, developed in the late 1970s, significantly influenced the integration of mindfulness into various mental health and therapeutic contexts, and we'll expand upon it in detail later in the chapter.

Mindfulness helps reduce stress, improve attention, decrease emotional reactivity, and increase cognitive flexibility. Regular practice can lead to changes in the brain associated with memory, empathy, and stress, and it's increasingly being employed in psychology to alleviate various mental and physical conditions.

THE SCIENCE BEHIND MINDFULNESS

The science behind mindfulness techniques is deeply rooted in understanding how these practices impact the brain and body, offering significant benefits that align well with the principles of somatic therapy.

NEUROLOGICAL IMPACT:

- **Brain Structure Changes:** Research using neuroimaging technology has shown that mindfulness practice can lead to changes in brain structure. Areas such as the prefrontal cortex, associated with higher-order brain functions like awareness, concentration, and decision-making, have been found to thicken with regular mindfulness practice.

- **Amygdala and Stress Response:** Mindfulness can reduce activity in the amygdala, the brain's fight or flight center, triggered during stress. This reduction can lead to decreased stress responses and a more balanced emotional state.

- **Enhanced Connectivity:** Mindfulness has been shown to enhance connectivity between different brain regions, improving functions like emotional regulation and introspection.

PHYSIOLOGICAL BENEFITS:

- **Reducing Stress Hormones**: Mindfulness practices can reduce levels of cortisol, the stress hormone. This reduction can alleviate symptoms related to stress and anxiety.

- **Autonomic Nervous System Regulation:** Mindfulness can help regulate the autonomic nervous system, balancing the sympathetic (fight or flight) and parasympathetic (rest and digest) nervous systems. This regulation is crucial in managing stress and promoting relaxation.

MINDFULNESS IN SOMATIC THERAPY:

- **Body Awareness:** Mindfulness enhances body awareness, a key component of somatic therapy. It helps clients tune into their bodily sensations and recognize how emotions are manifested physically.

- **Emotional Processing:** Observing one's thoughts and feelings without judgment (a core aspect of mindfulness) aligns with somatic therapy's approach to processing emotions. It allows individuals to safely explore and release stored emotions in the body.

- **Stress and Trauma Recovery:** Mindfulness techniques, by regulating stress responses and facilitating emotional regulation, complement somatic therapy's goal of healing trauma and stress-related disorders.

Somatic therapy's focus on bodily experiences can help clients achieve a deeper level of self-awareness, emotional processing, and overall well-being. This synergy makes mindfulness a powerful tool in somatic therapy, providing a scientific and practical foundation for its therapeutic applications.

BODY AWARENESS AND MINDFULNESS

The relationship between body awareness and mindfulness is intrinsically connected and mutually reinforcing. Both are key components in understanding and improving mental and physical well-being.

BODY AWARENESS:

- This refers to the conscious attention and sensitivity to the sensations, positions, movements, and overall state of one's body. It's about being in tune with physical experiences and recognizing signals like tension, pain, relaxation, or hunger.

- Body awareness is essential in identifying how emotions and stress manifest physically. For example, anxiety might be felt as a knot in the stomach or stress as tension in the shoulders.

MINDFULNESS:

- Mindfulness, as a focused attention and awareness practice, extends naturally to include body awareness. It involves observing thoughts, feelings, and bodily sensations in the present moment without judgment.

- A key aspect of mindfulness is paying attention to one's body. This can involve noticing the breath, the sensations in various parts of the body, or even the movement experience.

THE RELATIONSHIP:

- Mindfulness enhances body awareness. By practicing mindfulness, individuals learn to notice subtle physical sensations they might otherwise ignore. This increased awareness can lead to better understanding and management of emotions and stress, as physical sensations are often the first indicators of these states.

- Conversely, focusing on body awareness can enhance mindfulness. Paying attention to bodily sensations brings an individual into the present moment, a core aim of mindfulness. It grounds thoughts in the here and now, away from ruminations about the past or anxieties about the future.

- This relationship is leveraged to facilitate healing in therapeutic settings, particularly in somatic therapies. For instance, mindfulness-based stress reduction (MBSR) and mindfulness-based cognitive therapy (MBCT) use body awareness exercises as a key component of treatment.

Overall, the interplay between body awareness and mindfulness creates a powerful tool for self-awareness and self-regulation. It enables individuals to connect more deeply with themselves, offering more effective recovery.

ENHANCING BODY AWARENESS THROUGH MINDFULNESS TECHNIQUES

During somatic therapy, clients can expect to engage in various mindfulness practices designed to enhance body awareness and facilitate emotional processing. These practices help clients tune into their present-moment experiences, particularly focusing on bodily sensations and emotions. Here are some common mindfulness practices used in somatic therapy:

1. **Mindful Breathing:** This involves paying close attention to the breath and noticing the rhythm, depth, and quality of each breath. Mindful breathing helps to center the mind, reduce stress, and anchor the client in the present moment.

2. **Body Scan Meditation:** In this practice, clients are guided to mentally scan their body from head to toe, noticing any sensations, tensions, or discomforts. This practice promotes increased body awareness and helps identify areas where emotions might be stored.

3. **Grounding Exercises:** These exercises focus on connecting with the physical sensations of the body touching the ground or a chair. Grounding techniques can be particularly helpful in managing anxiety and dissociation, bringing the client back to the present.

4. **Movement Mindfulness:** This involves being aware of the body while in motion. It could include walking meditation, where the focus is on the sensation of each step or gentle stretching, emphasizing noticing the bodily sensations that arise with each movement.

5. **Mindful Observation of Emotions:** Clients are encouraged to observe their emotions without judgment, recognizing them as transient states. This practice fosters emotional regulation and helps clients understand the connection between their emotions and physical sensations.

6. **Focused Attention on Sensations:** Clients are guided to focus on specific physical sensations within their body. This could be tension, warmth, coolness, or tingling, which can reveal insights about emotional states.

7. **Guided Imagery:** This technique involves visualizing calming images or scenarios. It is often used with deep breathing to enhance relaxation and mental clarity.

8. **Journaling:** While not a traditional mindfulness practice, reflective writing can be a mindful activity when clients are encouraged to write about their present-moment thoughts and feelings, especially following a mindfulness exercise.

These mindfulness practices in somatic therapy enhance the mind-body connection, allowing clients to process emotions more effectively and develop greater self-awareness and resilience. They are integral tools for therapy sessions and clients to use in their daily lives to manage stress and emotional challenges.

Meditation Techniques for Healing Trauma

Meditation is a practice where an individual uses a technique – such as mindfulness, focusing their mind on a particular object, thought, or activity – to train attention and awareness and achieve a mentally clear and emotionally calm and stable state. It often involves sitting quietly and focusing on the breath, a word, or a phrase to quiet the mind. There are various forms of meditation, including concentration, which focuses on a single point, and open awareness, which involves observing thoughts or sensations that arise without attachment.

While meditation and mindfulness are closely related and often used interchangeably, they are distinct practices.

• **Meditation** is more of a formal practice. It typically involves setting aside time to engage in an activity (like sitting and focusing on the breath) that promotes a state of calm and centeredness.

Meditation is an umbrella term that encompasses various styles and techniques, including mindfulness meditation.

- **Mindfulness,** on the other hand, is a quality that can be brought to any activity. It's about being fully present and engaged in the moment, aware of your thoughts and feelings without judgment. Mindfulness can be practiced anytime – while eating, walking, or listening to someone. Mindfulness meditation is a form of meditation focused on cultivating this quality of awareness.

COMMON MISCONCEPTIONS ABOUT MEDITATION:

1. **"Meditation is about stopping your thoughts."** A common misconception is that the goal of meditation is to clear the mind of thoughts. However, meditation is more about noticing thoughts when they arise and learning to gently bring your focus back to your chosen point of attention.

2. **"You need to meditate for long periods for it to be effective."** While long meditation sessions can be beneficial, even short periods of meditation can be impactful. Consistency is often more important than duration.

3. **"Meditation is a religious practice."** While meditation has roots in religious traditions, it is widely practiced in secular contexts today. It is a tool for mental and emotional well-being and doesn't require any religious affiliation.

4. **"Meditation is only about relaxation."** While meditation can be deeply relaxing, its benefits extend beyond relaxation. It can enhance self-awareness, emotional regulation, and concentration, among other things.

5. **"Meditation is easy, or it should feel good all the time."** Meditation can sometimes be challenging. It can bring up uncomfortable emotions or thoughts, often requiring practice and discipline.

A greater look at these distinctions and misconceptions helps approach meditation and mindfulness with a more informed and open perspective, recognizing their unique roles in enhancing mental and emotional well-being.

MEDITATION'S VERSATILITY

With its diverse utilities, meditation has become a widespread technique incorporated into various recovery pathways, not just for mental health issues but also for broader wellness and self-improvement contexts. Its versatility and adaptability make it an effective tool across numerous settings:

1. **Stress Reduction:** One of the most common utilities of meditation is stress reduction. Regular meditation practice has been shown to decrease the production of stress hormones like cortisol and reduce the symptoms of stress-related disorders.

2. **Emotional Well-being and Mental Health:** Meditation can improve emotional well-being, reducing symptoms of anxiety and depression. It helps individuals develop skills to manage their emotions, leading to enhanced mood stability and overall mental health.

3. **Trauma Recovery:** In the context of trauma recovery, certain forms of meditation can be beneficial. Practices like mindfulness meditation help individuals stay grounded in the present moment, which can be particularly useful for those dealing with PTSD or past trauma.

4. **Substance Abuse and Addiction Recovery:** Meditation is increasingly being used in programs for substance abuse and addiction recovery. It aids in developing self-control, mindfulness, and awareness of triggers, which are crucial in the recovery process.

5. **Chronic Pain Management:** Meditation is effective in managing chronic pain. It helps alter the perception of pain and can be an integral part of a comprehensive pain management strategy.

6. **Improved Focus and Cognition:** Regular meditation practice has been associated with improved attention, concentration, and overall cognitive function. It can enhance memory, creativity, and problem-solving skills.

7. **Sleep Improvement:** Meditation can improve sleep quality, helping with conditions like insomnia. Meditation can be a valuable tool in improving sleep patterns by promoting relaxation and helping to control the racing thoughts that often lead to sleep disturbances.

8. **Physical Health:** Beyond mental health, meditation has been linked to improved physical health. It can benefit cardiovascular health by reducing heart rate and blood pressure and has been associated with a lower risk of certain diseases.

9. **Spiritual Growth:** For many, meditation also serves as a path to spiritual growth and self-realization. It can be integral to various spiritual and religious practices, helping individuals connect more deeply with their beliefs.

Incorporated into therapies like Mindfulness-Based Stress Reduction (MBSR), Mindfulness-Based Cognitive Therapy (MBCT), and various other integrative health approaches, meditation's widespread utility across different recovery pathways highlights its effectiveness as a holistic healing and well-being tool. Its ability to be adapted and tailored to meet various needs makes it a versatile and valuable component in health and wellness, and more so for somatic therapy.

HEALING TRAUMA THROUGH MEDITATION

In the context of using somatic therapy to heal trauma, meditation techniques are tailored to help clients reconnect with their bodies and process traumatic experiences in a safe and controlled manner. The focus is on techniques that enhance body awareness and regulate the nervous system, which is essential for trauma recovery. Here are some meditation techniques a client can expect in somatic therapy for trauma healing:

1. **Grounding Meditation:** This involves practices that help clients feel more grounded and present in their bodies. Techniques might include focusing on the sensation of feet touching the ground, the weight of the body on a chair, or the touch of hands on the lap. Grounding meditations are particularly useful for clients who experience dissociation or feel overwhelmed by traumatic memories.

2. **Mindful Breathing:** Clients are guided to focus on their breath, observing the inhalation and exhalation and the way their body moves with each breath. This technique helps regulate the nervous system and can be calming for those experiencing anxiety or hyperarousal symptoms associated with trauma.

3. Body Scan Meditation: In this practice, attention is slowly moved through different parts of the body, noting any sensations, tensions, or numbness. Body scan meditations help in developing deeper body awareness, a crucial aspect for clients who may have disconnected from their bodies due to trauma.

4. Progressive Muscle Relaxation (PMR): PMR involves tensing and then relaxing different muscle groups in the body. This practice can help clients identify areas where they hold trauma-related tension and learn to release it.

5. Mindful Movement: Techniques such as gentle yoga or Tai Chi can be integrated. These practices involve slow, deliberate movements combined with breath awareness, helping clients reconnect with their bodies in a safe and mindful way.

6. Guided Visualization: Clients might be guided through visualizations that promote a sense of safety and calm. This can include imagining a safe place or visualizing the release of trauma from the body.

7. Compassion-Focused Meditation: Especially useful for clients who struggle with self-criticism or shame as a result of trauma, these meditations cultivate self-compassion and kindness towards oneself.

8. Trauma-Sensitive Mindfulness: Adapted to be safe for trauma survivors, these practices ensure that clients are not overwhelmed during meditation. They emphasize the client's control over the process and the ability to disengage from practices that might trigger traumatic memories.

In somatic therapy for trauma, meditation is used not just as a relaxation tool but as a means to gently process and integrate traumatic experiences. These techniques are introduced gradually and mindfully, always respecting the client's pace and ensuring they feel safe and supported throughout the process.

Mindfulness-Based Stress Reduction (MBSR) Strategies

Mindfulness-Based Stress Reduction (MBSR) is a structured therapeutic program designed to reduce stress and improve mental and physical health through mindfulness practices. Developed by Dr. Jon Kabat-Zinn in the late 1970s at the University of Massachusetts Medical Center, MBSR combines mindfulness meditation, body awareness, and yoga to help people become more aware of their thoughts, feelings, and bodily sensations in a non-judgmental way.

KEY COMPONENTS OF MBSR:

1. **Mindfulness Meditation:** Central to the program, these practices involve focusing on the present moment and observing thoughts and feelings as they arise without trying to change or judge them.

2. **Body Scan:** A guided meditation that involves paying attention to various parts of the body, noting any sensations or discomforts, and cultivating awareness of the body's physical state.

3. **Gentle Yoga:** Yoga practices included in MBSR are designed to improve awareness of bodily sensations, increase flexibility, and reduce stress.

4. **Group Discussions:** Participants engage in group discussions where they share experiences and learn from each other's insights into mindfulness practices.

5. **Daily Home Practice:** Participants are encouraged to practice mindfulness techniques independently. This home practice is a critical part of the program, as it helps integrate mindfulness into everyday life.

GOALS AND BENEFITS:

- The primary goal of MBSR is to help participants become more aware of their thoughts, feelings, and body sensations and to learn how to respond to them in a non-reactive, mindful way.

- MBSR has been shown to reduce symptoms of stress, anxiety, and depression. It's also been beneficial in managing chronic pain, improving sleep quality, and enhancing overall well-being.

- The program is designed to teach participants skills that can help them cope better with stress and adversity.

RESEARCH AND EFFECTIVENESS:

- MBSR has been the subject of extensive research since its inception. Studies have shown that it can lead to significant reductions in psychological and physiological symptoms of stress.

- It has been adapted for various populations, including corporate employees, students, prisoners, and patients with various health conditions.

MBSR is not just a stress-reduction program; it's a way to learn about and transform one's relationship with experiences, leading to a higher quality of life. It's particularly effective because it combines ancient mindfulness practices with contemporary psychological understanding.

PROGRAM ROUTINE

The structure of the Mindfulness-Based Stress Reduction (MBSR) program is carefully designed to teach participants mindfulness practices and integrate them into daily life. It is an 8-week program that consists of several key components:

1. Weekly Classes: The program includes weekly group sessions, each lasting approximately 2.5 hours. A trained MBSR instructor leads these sessions and typically consist of guided mindfulness practices, group discussions, and exercises. Participants are introduced to various aspects of mindfulness and are encouraged to share their experiences and challenges related to the practices.

2. Daily Home Practice: A significant component of MBSR is the commitment to daily mindfulness practice at home. Participants are typically given assignments that include various forms of meditation (like sitting meditation, body scans, or walking meditation) and gentle yoga exercises. This daily practice, usually recommended for about 45 minutes daily, is crucial for developing and strengthening mindfulness skills.

3. **All-Day Retreat:** There is an all-day retreat around the sixth or seventh week of the program. This retreat, which often lasts around 7-8 hours, provides an intensive opportunity for deepening mindfulness practice in a supportive group setting. It's a silent retreat focusing on meditation practices learned during the course.

4. **Educational Components:** The program includes teachings on the theory and principles of mindfulness, stress physiology, and applying mindfulness in stressful situations. These teachings are integrated into the weekly sessions and aim to better understand how mindfulness works and its benefits.

5. **Interactive Learning:** The program is experiential and participatory. Group discussions and sharing of experiences are integral parts, allowing participants to learn from each other and feel supported by the group.

6. **Guided Instructions:** Participants receive guided instructions in various mindfulness practices throughout the program. These include mindfulness meditation, where the focus is placed on the breath or bodily sensations, and mindful movement practices, like yoga or stretching exercises, to cultivate awareness of bodily sensations.

7. **Integration into Daily Life:** A key goal of the program is to help participants integrate mindfulness into their everyday activities. This is encouraged through "informal" practices like mindful eating, mindful walking, or mindful listening.

The MBSR program's structured approach is designed to progressively build and integrate mindfulness skills into daily life. This structure supports the development of a personal mindfulness practice that can be sustained beyond the duration of the program, providing long-term benefits for stress management and overall well-being.

Chapter Summary

Throughout our exploration of somatic therapy, mindfulness, and meditation, we've delved into various therapeutic practices and concepts that contribute significantly to healing and recovery. We began by examining the principles of somatic therapy, a holistic approach focusing on the mind-body connection and emphasizing the physical manifestations of emotional experiences. Techniques like body scanning, mindful breathing, and progressive muscle relaxation were discussed as key components of this therapy.

We then transitioned to exploring mindfulness and meditation, shedding light on their scientific underpinnings and therapeutic benefits. Mindfulness-Based Stress Reduction (MBSR) was highlighted as a structured program integrating mindfulness into stress management and overall well-being. The significance of meditation in various forms and its utility across different recovery pathways was also examined, underscoring its versatility and adaptability.

In addition, we discussed the importance of self-compassion in the recovery process, recognizing that kindness and understanding towards oneself are vital for healing. The role of emotional triggers and patterns in shaping our responses to stress and trauma was explored, emphasizing the need for awareness and management of these elements.

As we conclude this chapter, it's clear that the integration of body and mind is central to these therapeutic approaches. Each topic discussed contributes to a deeper understanding of how our mental, emotional, and physical states are interconnected and how we can harness this connection for healing.

Moving to the next part, we will delve further into this interplay, focusing on strengthening the mind-body connection. Furthermore, we will build upon our current understanding, exploring advanced techniques and practices that enhance the connection and leverage it for deeper healing and personal growth.

My Note

PART 3

Strengthening the Mind-Body Connection

Chapter 10

Daily Practices for Wellness

In this vital chapter, we focus on establishing morning, daily, and evening routines that are specifically designed to help individuals cope with the challenges of trauma and chronic stress. How we start our day, manage our daily activities, and wind down in the evening can significantly impact our well-being, and this chapter is dedicated to providing structured, practical strategies that can be integrated into everyday life. These routines are crafted to foster resilience, promote healing, and provide a sense of stability and control, which are often compromised in the wake of trauma and chronic stress.

We begin with the morning routine, understanding that the start of the day sets the tone for the following hours. This section will offer techniques and practices to begin the day with a sense of calm, purpose, and positivity, even amidst the challenges of trauma and stress.

Moving into the daily routine, we recognize that the core of our day can often bring unpredictability and stressors. Here, we will explore strategies for maintaining a balanced state of mind, managing stressors effectively, and incorporating mindfulness and self-care practices into daily activities.

Finally, the evening routine will focus on practices that help in winding down and transitioning into a restful, healing sleep. This part of the routine is crucial for processing the day's events, calming the nervous system, and preparing the body and mind for rejuvenation.

Throughout this chapter, we will emphasize therapeutic, feasible, and adaptable to various lifestyles and needs. Whether you are navigating the aftermath of trauma or dealing with the persistent pressure of chronic stress, these routines can offer a guiding framework to support your journey toward recovery and well-being. Let's embark on creating these routines, each tailored to nurture your resilience and aid your healing process.

Morning Rituals for Grounding and Centering

The importance of utilizing the morning to set the right tone for the rest of the day cannot be overstated, especially for individuals coping with trauma or chronic stress. Mornings are more than just the start of the day; they are an instrumental period that can significantly influence our mindset, emotional state, and overall effectiveness. Here's why establishing a positive and mindful morning routine is so impactful:

- **Setting a Positive Tone:** How we start our day often sets the tone for the following hours. A calm, centered, and positive morning can lead to a more balanced and productive day. It can help cultivate a mindset better equipped to handle stress and challenges.

- **Cultivating Mindfulness:** Engaging in mindfulness practices in the morning, such as meditation or mindful breathing, can help center the mind, reduce morning anxiety, and increase awareness and focus. This heightened mindfulness can improve our ability to respond to situations thoughtfully rather than reactively throughout the day.

- **Building Resilience:** A morning routine with stress-reduction practices can enhance emotional resilience. By starting the day in a state of calm and equilibrium, we are better prepared to face stressors with a grounded and stable mindset.

- **Enhancing Mental Clarity:** A clear and focused mind is more capable of decision-making and problem-solving. Morning routines that include journaling, planning, or even light exercise can boost cognitive function and mental clarity.

- **Establishing Control:** For those dealing with trauma or chronic stress, a structured morning routine can create a sense of control and predictability, which is often needed in the healing process. It provides an anchor, reducing feelings of chaos or uncertainty that can be prevalent in these situations.

- **Self-Care and Compassion:** Prioritizing self-care in the morning demonstrates self-compassion and respect for one's needs. This can be particularly empowering for recovering from trauma, as it reinforces a positive self-relationship and personal worth.

- **Physical Health Benefits:** Engaging in morning activities like stretching, yoga, or a healthy breakfast can positively affect physical health, which in turn supports mental health and stress management.

Approach the morning as a powerful opportunity to lay a foundation of positivity, resilience, and mindfulness that supports mental and emotional well-being throughout the day. For those coping with trauma or chronic stress, a mindful and structured morning routine is a significant step toward healing and recovery.

COMMON CHALLENGES OF ESTABLISHING MORNING RITUALS

Establishing morning rituals can be challenging for many people, and these challenges can vary based on individual circumstances, lifestyle, and specific stressors or trauma they might be dealing with. Common challenges include:

1. **Lack of Time:** Many people feel they don't have enough time in the morning for additional activities. Busy schedules, especially for those with family or work obligations, can make it difficult to carve out time for morning rituals.

2. **Consistency:** Developing a new routine and sticking to it consistently can be challenging. It often requires discipline and a change inhabits, which can take time and effort.

3. **Fatigue and Sleep Issues:** For those who struggle with sleep problems, whether it's difficulty falling asleep, staying asleep, or waking up feeling unrested, mustering the energy for morning rituals can be tough.

4. **Overwhelmed:** Deciding what rituals to include in the morning routine can be overwhelming, especially with the abundance of advice and recommendations available. People may struggle to find what works best for them.

5. **Motivation:** On some days, particularly for those dealing with stress or trauma, finding the motivation to engage in morning rituals can be challenging. Emotional and mental health issues can impact one's drive and energy.

6. **Distractions:** Distractions, such as technology, can impede the establishment of focused and mindful morning rituals. The temptation to check emails or social media first thing in the morning can derail attempts to start the day mindfully.

7. **Physical Limitations or Health Issues:** For some individuals, physical health issues or limitations can make it challenging to engage in certain types of morning rituals, especially those that involve physical activity.

8. **Lack of Immediate Results:** Some people may become discouraged if they don't see immediate benefits from their morning rituals. Establishing new habits often requires patience and persistence.

9. **Cultural or Familial Expectations:** Sometimes, cultural or family norms and expectations can make it difficult to prioritize personal morning rituals, especially if others do not understand or value them in one's environment.

10. **Stress and Anxiety:** For individuals dealing with chronic stress or anxiety, the act of adding another task to their morning, even if it's intended to be beneficial, can initially feel like an additional source of stress.

The key to successfully establishing morning rituals lies in taking these challenges head-on. This often involves starting with small, manageable practices, being patient with oneself, and experimenting to find what truly resonates and feels beneficial.

GROUNDING AND CENTERING IN THE MORNING

In somatic therapy, morning rituals for grounding and centering are important practices that help individuals start their day with a strong sense of physical and emotional stability. These rituals are especially beneficial for those dealing with trauma or chronic stress, as they foster a connection between the body and mind, providing a solid foundation for the day ahead.

Grounding refers to practices that connect an individual to the present moment, primarily through physical sensations. The goal is to anchor oneself in the "here and now," which can be particularly helpful in managing symptoms of trauma and anxiety that often involve feeling disconnected from the present or being overwhelmed by past experiences. Grounding techniques might include walking barefoot to feel the texture of the ground, engaging in a body scan meditation to attentively move through and notice sensations in different parts of the body, or practicing mindful breathing while focusing on the sensation of breath entering and leaving the body. These practices bring awareness back to the physical body and can help alleviate feelings of disconnection, anxiety, or emotional gravity.

Centering, on the other hand, involves aligning one's emotional and mental state, creating a sense of inner balance and calm. Centering practices often include setting intentions for the day, engaging in mindfulness meditation, or practicing gentle yoga or tai chi. These activities help cultivate an inner sense of peace and stability, allowing individuals to approach their day with clarity and purpose. Centering helps in managing emotional responses and fosters resilience against daily stressors.

Both grounding and centering are vital in somatic therapy, as they address the connection between the mind and body, which is often disrupted in trauma and chronic stress. Integrating these practices into morning rituals can significantly influence an individual's ability to navigate the day with greater control, calmness, and emotional equilibrium.

The ideal morning times for practicing grounding and centering techniques can vary based on individual schedules and preferences. However, incorporating these practices into the early part of your morning routine is most effective. Here are some suggestions:

1. GROUNDING PRACTICES: Ideal time - Shortly after waking up.

- Aim to engage in grounding techniques soon after you wake up. This could be within the first 15 to 30 minutes of your morning.

- If possible, you might start with a simple 5-10 minute barefoot walk outside to connect physically with the earth.

- Alternatively, a brief body scan meditation can be very grounding, focusing on the sensations in different parts of your body while still in bed or shortly after getting out of bed.

- The key is to do this before the day's activities and distractions begin, setting a stable foundation for the day.

2. CENTERING PRACTICES: Ideal time - As part of your morning routine.

- Centering activities such as setting intentions, mindfulness meditation, or gentle yoga can be incorporated as you progress into your morning routine, perhaps after a shower or breakfast.

- This could be approximately 30 to 60 minutes after waking, allowing flexibility based on your overall morning schedule.

- A 10–20-minute session of centering practices can be highly effective. It can be done in a quiet space where you are unlikely to be interrupted.

- Including centering practices after some initial waking, activities can help ensure you are fully awake and more receptive to the mental and emotional alignment these exercises offer.

It's important to remember that consistency is key. A few minutes dedicated regularly to these practices can be more beneficial than longer, sporadic sessions. Adapting the timing to fit comfortably into your morning routine will make it more sustainable and effective in the long run.

Integrating Somatic Techniques into Daily Life

DAILY LIFE HABITS EXPLAINED

In coping with trauma or chronic stress, "daily life" practices refer to the habits, activities, and routines that individuals integrate into their regular day-to-day lives to manage symptoms, promote healing, and maintain overall well-being. These practices are key components of a holistic approach to recovery and self-care. They involve consciously incorporating certain behaviors and mindsets into various aspects of one's daily routine.

The power of these practices lies in their ability to transform habits – the regular tendencies or practices that we often perform automatically. Habits are powerful because they shape a significant portion of our daily life without us being fully aware of it. Individuals can significantly influence their mental, emotional, and physical health by developing positive, health-promoting habits. Here's a small guide to building powerful habits:

1. Consistency and Routine: Habits are formed through repetition. These actions become more automatic by consistently practicing beneficial activities, like mindfulness, exercise, or healthy eating. This consistency helps stabilize mood and reduce stress as the body and mind come to anticipate and rely on these positive routines.

2. **Incremental Change:** The power of habits also lies in their ability to bring about incremental but sustainable change. Small daily practices can accumulate over time, leading to significant long-term benefits in coping with trauma and stress.

3. **Cognitive and Emotional Regulation:** Daily life practices can help regulate cognitive and emotional responses. For instance, regular mindfulness practice can alter habitual patterns of thought that contribute to anxiety and stress, leading to more balanced emotional responses.

4. **Physical Health:** Daily habits also directly impact physical health. Activities like regular exercise, adequate sleep, and balanced nutrition not only improve physical well-being but also contribute to better mental health.

5. **Sense of Control:** Establishing positive daily practices can provide a sense of control and predictability, which is often needed in the face of trauma and chronic stress. This sense of control can empower individuals to deal with uncertainty and helplessness.

6. **Building Resilience:** Over time, these practices contribute to building resilience. They equip individuals with tools and skills to better handle stressors and bounce back from difficult experiences.

SOMATIC TECHNIQUES FOR DAILY LIFE

You are not limited to the therapy sessions. Practicing somatic therapy techniques at home can be valuable in managing stress, processing emotions, and enhancing body awareness. Here are some techniques that you can easily incorporate into your daily routine:

1. **Mindful Breathing:** This is a fundamental somatic exercise. Focus on your breath, noticing the sensations as you inhale and exhale. Breathe deeply into your abdomen and observe how it rises and

falls. This practice helps regulate the nervous system and brings attention to the present moment.

2. **Body Scan Meditation:** Lie in a comfortable position and slowly bring your attention to different parts of your body. Notice any sensations, tension, or discomfort. This technique increases body awareness and helps identify areas where you might be holding stress.

3. **Grounding Exercises:** These exercises help you connect with the present moment. Try standing barefoot and feeling the ground beneath your feet or sitting and noticing the sensations where your body touches the chair. Grounding can be particularly helpful in moments of anxiety or disconnection.

4. **Progressive Muscle Relaxation (PMR):** Systematically tense and then relax different muscle groups. Start from your toes and move upwards. This helps release muscle tension and brings awareness to physical sensations in the body.

5. **Gentle Movement or Stretching:** Engage in slow, mindful movements or stretches. Pay attention to how each movement feels in your body. Yoga or Tai Chi can be excellent practices for integrating mindful movement.

6. **Pendulation:** Notice any sensations of discomfort or tension in your body. Then, shift your attention to a part of your body that feels more neutral or pleasant. Alternating (pendulating) between these sensations can help manage and process difficult bodily sensations.

7. **Mindful Walking:** Go for a walk and focus on the experience of walking. Notice the sensation of each foot as it touches the ground, the rhythm of your steps, and how your body feels as it moves.

8. **Journaling:** After engaging in these somatic exercises, take some time to journal about your experience. Note any sensations, emotions, and thoughts that arose during the practice.

To simplify, these are just abridged, lite versions of the therapeutic techniques your therapist will encourage you to practice during your sessions. The key to these practices is mindfulness – the act of paying attention on purpose, in the present moment, non-judgmentally.

Start with short sessions and gradually increase the duration as you become more comfortable with the practices. These techniques can be a valuable addition to your self-care routine, connecting with your body's wisdom and cultivating a sense of inner balance.

TIME RECOMMENDATIONS

For the remaining times of the day, outside of morning and evening routines, integrating somatic therapy techniques can be highly beneficial. It can be tailored to suit individual schedules and needs. Here are some suggestions for ideal times to practice these techniques:

1. MID-MORNING (AROUND 10:00 AM - 11:00 AM):

• After the initial rush of the morning, a mid-morning break can be a perfect time for a brief body scan or mindful breathing session. This can help in re-centering and managing any stress that may have accumulated since the start of the day.

2. LUNCH BREAK (AROUND 12:00 PM - 2:00 PM):

• Utilize a part of your lunch break for grounding exercises. This can be especially useful to counteract the sedentary nature of desk jobs. A short walk, focusing on the sensation of your feet touching the ground, can be rejuvenating.

3. MID-AFTERNOON (AROUND 3:00 PM - 4:00 PM):

• This is often when energy levels dip. Engage in gentle stretching or mindful movement, like Tai Chi or yoga, to revitalize your body and mind. This can also help maintain focus and productivity for the rest of the day.

4. LATE AFTERNOON/PRE-EVENING (AROUND 5:00 PM - 6:00 PM):

• As the workday winds down, progressive muscle relaxation can help release any physical tension built up over the day. This can also serve as a transition activity, marking the end of work and the beginning of personal time.

5. POST-DINNER (AROUND 7:00 PM - 8:00 PM):

• After dinner can be an opportune time for a mindful walk. This not only aids digestion but also offers a chance to practice mindfulness and enjoy the transition into the evening.

6. BEFORE BEDTIME ROUTINE (AROUND 9:00 PM):

• Before starting your evening routine, take some time to journal about your day, focusing on your bodily sensations and emotional states. This reflection can promote self-awareness and relaxation.

These times are just guidelines and can be adjusted based on your schedule and preferences. The key is to find moments throughout the day when you can pause and reconnect with your body and mind, which can be particularly beneficial for maintaining emotional balance and managing stress; it can be as small as 3-5 minutes.

Evening Routines for Relaxation and Reflection

For evening routines, focusing on relaxation and reflection is essential, especially in the context of managing stress and trauma. These practices can help unwind from the day's activities, processing any emotional experiences during the day, and preparing for restful sleep. Here are some key elements to consider for an evening routine centered around relaxation and reflection:

1. **Mindful Unwinding:** Transition from your day to evening by engaging in a mindful unwinding process. This could include changing into comfortable clothes, dimming the lights, or listening to soothing music. The aim is to signal your body and mind that it's time to slow down.

2. **Reflective Journaling:** Set aside time to journal about your day. Focus on noting any significant events, how you felt, what you learned, and how you handled various situations. Journaling is a

powerful tool for reflection and processing emotions.

3. **Gentle Yoga or Stretching:** Incorporate gentle yoga poses or stretching into your evening routine. This practice can help release physical tension in the body and calm the mind. Focus on slow, mindful movements, paying attention to your breathing.

4. **Guided Relaxation or Meditation:** Engage in a guided relaxation or meditation session. There are many online resources and apps available for guided practice. Choose sessions that emphasize relaxation and letting go of the day's stress.

5. **Gratitude Practice:** Reflect on and write down three things you are grateful for from your day. Gratitude practice can shift your focus from stressors to positive aspects of your life, fostering a sense of contentment and well-being.

6. **Breathing Exercises:** Practice deep breathing or specific breathing techniques like the 4-7-8 method. Breathing exercises effectively activate the parasympathetic nervous system, promoting relaxation, and preparing the body for sleep.

7. **Warm Bath or Shower:** A warm bath or shower can be relaxing and is an excellent way to mark the end of the day physically and mentally. You can use this time to practice mindfulness, focusing on the sensation of the water.

8. **Prepare for the Next Day:** To reduce anxiety and promote a relaxed state of mind, spend a few minutes preparing for the next day. This might involve setting out clothes, planning your to-do list, or preparing lunch. The idea is to do these tasks mindfully, without rushing.

9. **Relaxing Bedtime Ritual:** Create a bedtime ritual that promotes relaxation. This could include reading a book, practicing a few minutes of meditation, or simply lying in bed and doing a body scan to relax each part of your body.

10. **Digital Detox:** Aim to disconnect from digital devices at least 30 minutes before bedtime. The blue light from screens can interfere with the production of melatonin, a hormone that regulates sleep.

You don't have to engage in all the practices. Choose the ones that resonate with you and make them a regular part of your evening to reap the full benefits. This routine is not just about ending the day but also about setting the tone for a peaceful night and a positive start to the next morning, creating an emotionally regulating night-day cycle.

Additional Habits

In addition to specific morning and evening routines, incorporating additional habits into your daily routine can significantly enhance your ability to cope with trauma and chronic stress. These habits can provide steady support throughout the day, reinforcing the benefits of targeted morning and evening practices. Here are some habits that can complement your daily routine:

1. **Regular Physical Activity:** Engage in regular exercise or physical activity, such as walking, jogging, cycling, or yoga. Physical exercise is good for the body and helps release endorphins, which are natural mood lifters.

2. **Mindful Eating:** Practice mindful eating by paying attention to your food's taste, texture, and sensations. This habit helps improve digestion and create a more mindful relationship with food and eating habits.

3. **Scheduled Breaks:** Incorporate short, regular breaks throughout your day, especially if you have a sedentary job. Use these breaks for stretching, a brief walk, or a short mindfulness or breathing exercise.

4. **Nature Connection:** Spend time in nature whenever possible. This could be a walk in a park, gardening, or sitting in a natural setting. Connecting with nature can have a calming effect on the mind and body.

5. **Hydration and Nutrition:** Maintain a habit of staying hydrated and eating balanced, nutritious meals. Proper nutrition and hydration are crucial for mental and physical health.

6. **Mindfulness Practices:** Integrate brief mindfulness practices throughout the day. This could be as simple as taking a few mindful breaths between tasks or practicing mindfulness meditation during your lunch break.

7. **Social Interaction:** Make time for positive social interactions, whether in conversation with a colleague, calling a friend, or spending quality time with family. Positive social support is essential for emotional well-being.

8. **Creative Outlets:** Engage in creative activities like drawing, writing, playing music, or crafting. Creative expression can be therapeutic and a great way to process emotions.

9. **Limiting Screen Time:** Be mindful of your screen time, especially social media and news exposure. Excessive screen time can lead to increased stress and distraction.

10. **Practicing Gratitude:** Take a few moments each day to reflect on things you are grateful for. Gratitude practice can shift your focus from negative to positive aspects of life, enhancing overall well-being.

These habits, woven into your daily life, can provide a strong foundation for managing stress and trauma.

Showcasing a Daily Wellness Schedule

Let's follow a day in the life of Mia, who has been using morning, daily, and evening routines to manage her stress and recover from past trauma:

MORNING:

6:30 AM: Mia wakes up and immediately practices a grounding exercise, feeling the floor under her feet as she stands up. She then spends a few minutes doing a body scan meditation, noticing any tension and breathing into those areas.

7:00 AM: Mia spends 10 minutes in mindful breathing after her shower, focusing on each inhale and exhale to center her thoughts for the day.

7:30 AM: Mia practices mindful eating during breakfast, savoring her food and focusing on the flavors and textures.

DAILY ROUTINE:

10:00 AM: Mid-morning at work, Mia takes a 5-minute break for deep breathing exercises at her desk, helping her refocus and release any building tension.

12:30 PM: During lunch, Mia goes for a 20-minute mindful walk outside, feeling the sun on her skin and the rhythm of her steps, reconnecting with her body and nature.

3:00 PM: Mia takes a short break for stretching, doing gentle yoga poses to release physical tension and refresh her mind.

5:30 PM: Before leaving work, Mia spends a few minutes planning her tasks for the next day, helping her mentally close the workday and transition to personal time.

EVENING:

6:30 PM: After dinner, Mia engages in reflective journaling, writing about her day's experiences, emotions, and learnings.

7:30 PM: Mia practices a gratitude exercise, listing three things she is grateful for from the day, fostering positivity.

8:00 PM: Mia winds down with a guided relaxation meditation, helping her release any remaining stress and prepare for sleep.

9:30 PM: Before bed, Mia reads a book for 30 minutes, a digital detox routine that helps her relax and signals her body that it's time to sleep.

Through this structured yet flexible routine, Mia successfully navigates her day with a focus on mindfulness and self-care, effectively managing her stress and trauma recovery. This schedule provides her with a sense of control and stability and integrates therapeutic practices into her everyday life, contributing to her overall well-being.

Chapter Summary

In conclusion, this chapter has outlined a comprehensive approach to creating morning, daily, and evening routines aimed at managing trauma and chronic stress. As we have seen through Mia's example, integrating specific practices into each part of the day can significantly enhance one's ability to cope with stress, process emotions, and maintain a sense of equilibrium.

The morning routines set a tone of mindfulness and grounding, enabling a start to the day that is centered and focused. The daily routines provide structured breaks for rejuvenation and stress management, which is crucial for maintaining balance amid the day's challenges. Finally, the evening routines offer opportunities for reflection, relaxation, and preparation for restorative sleep, which is essential for mental and physical health.

Adopting such routines doesn't require drastic changes but rather a series of small, manageable adjustments that can be tailored to individual lifestyles and needs. The key is consistency and mindfulness in these practices, allowing the benefits to accumulate and contribute to a more resilient and peaceful state of being.

My Note

Chapter 11

Holistic Approaches to Somatic Healing

Your road to recovery should not be limited to therapy sessions. In this insightful chapter, we broaden our scope to explore holistic healing, recognizing that true recovery from trauma and stress often requires an integration of various approaches beyond somatic therapy alone. Holistic healing acknowledges that every aspect of a person's life - body, mind, and spirit - contributes to their overall well-being. Here, we will delve into three key components that can complement somatic therapy: nutrition, yoga, and expressive arts. Each offers unique benefits and works synergistically to support the healing process.

We begin with how our foods can impact our mental and physical health. Nutrition plays a crucial role in healing from trauma and managing stress, as certain foods can either exacerbate or alleviate stress responses in the body. We'll discuss dietary choices that support the body's natural healing processes, improve mood, and enhance energy levels.

Next, we focus on yoga, a practice combining physical postures, breathwork, and meditation. Yoga is an invaluable tool for healing, offering a way to reconnect with the body, release stored tension, and cultivate a sense of inner peace. We'll explore different styles of yoga and how they can be tailored to individual needs and experiences, particularly in the context of trauma and stress.

Finally, we will explore the therapeutic power of expressive arts. These activities provide an outlet for expressing emotions and experiences that might be difficult to articulate verbally. Expressive arts can foster creativity, self-expression, and emotional release, contributing to the holistic healing journey.

This chapter will provide a comprehensive understanding of these complementary practices and how they can be integrated into your healing journey. By approaching healing holistically, we open ourselves to many pathways that can nurture our journey toward recovery and well-being. Let's begin.

Nutrition and Its Impact on Mental Health: A Holistic Perspective

Nutrition refers to providing or obtaining the food necessary for health and growth. It's a vital component of health and development, affecting all aspects of human life. Proper nutrition involves consuming a balanced diet rich in vitamins, minerals, and other nutrients essential for the body's functioning. This includes carbohydrates, proteins, fats, vitamins, and minerals. These nutrients are required for various bodily functions like energy production, immune response, cellular repair, and overall maintenance of bodily systems. The quality and type of food we consume directly impact our physical health, mental well-being, and ability to recover from illnesses and stress. In holistic health approaches, such as somatic therapy, nutrition plays a crucial role in supporting the body's natural healing processes and maintaining the balance between physical and mental health.

Nutrition is broadly categorized into macronutrients and micronutrients, each playing specific and crucial roles in the body:

1. MACRONUTRIENTS - These are nutrients required in larger quantities in our diet. They are the primary source of energy and essential for growth, metabolism, and other bodily functions.

- **Carbohydrates:** They are the body's main energy source. Carbohydrates break down into glucose, which the body's cells use for energy. They are essential for brain function and are found in foods like grains, fruits, and vegetables.

- **Proteins:** Proteins are vital for building and repairing tissues, including muscles, skin, and organs. They also play a key role in making enzymes, hormones, and other body chemicals. Protein is found in meat, fish, dairy products, beans, and nuts.

- **Fats:** Fats are a concentrated energy source necessary for various functions, such as nutrient absorption, nerve transmission, and maintaining cell membrane integrity. They come in different forms, including saturated, unsaturated, and trans fats, found in oils, butter, avocado, and fatty fish.

2. MICRONUTRIENTS - These are nutrients needed in smaller amounts but are essential for preventing disease and supporting well-being and development.

- **Vitamins:** These are organic compounds necessary for various metabolic processes. For example, Vitamin C is crucial for immune function and skin health, Vitamin D for bone health and immune response, and B vitamins for energy metabolism and brain function.

- **Minerals:** These are inorganic elements that play roles in a wide range of bodily functions. Calcium is essential for bone health, iron is crucial for blood production and oxygen transport, and potassium regulates fluid balance and nerve signals.

Each macro and micronutrient has specific functions and contributes to the body's overall well-being. A balanced diet containing various foods is generally the best way to ensure adequate intake of these essential nutrients. In somatic therapy, understanding and optimizing the intake of these nutrients can significantly enhance the body's ability to manage stress, heal from trauma, and maintain overall mental and physical health.

NUTRITION AND MENTAL HEALTH

Nutrition has both overt and covert impacts on mental health, influencing our well-being in multiple, sometimes subtle, ways:

OVERT IMPACTS:

- **Mood Regulation:** Certain nutrients directly influence brain chemistry and mood. For example, omega-3 fatty acids, found in fatty fish, have been linked to reduced rates of depression.

- **Cognitive Function:** Nutritional deficiencies, particularly in vitamins B, D, and omega-3 fatty acids, can lead to diminished cognitive functioning, affecting memory, attention, and problem-solving skills.

- **Energy Levels:** Macronutrients like carbohydrates are critical for energy. Inadequate or imbalanced intake can lead to fatigue, affecting mental alertness and overall mood.

- **Sleep Quality:** Diet affects sleep patterns. For instance, high caffeine or sugar consumption can disrupt sleep, impacting mental health.

COVERT IMPACTS:

- **Gut-Brain Axis:** The gut microbiome significantly affects mental health. A diet rich in fiber, probiotics, and a balance of nutrients supports a healthy gut linked to reduced anxiety and depression.

- **Inflammation:** Chronic inflammation, which can be exacerbated by poor nutrition, is linked to a higher risk of mental health disorders.

Anti-inflammatory foods like leafy greens and berries can help mitigate this risk.

- **Stress Response:** Nutritional status can influence the body's response to stress. Certain minerals like magnesium, found in nuts and leafy greens, regulate the stress response.

- **Long-term Health Risks:** Poor nutrition over time can lead to chronic health conditions like obesity and diabetes, which are linked to higher rates of depression and anxiety.

The complex relationship between nutrition and mental health in somatic therapy underscores the need for a holistic approach to health, where dietary habits are considered alongside physical and psychological therapies for comprehensive well-being.

A QUICK NUTRITIONAL GUIDE

To harness nutrition for both physical and mental health benefits, it's essential to focus on a balanced and mindful approach to eating. Here are some guidelines:

1. BALANCED DIET:

- **Incorporate Variety:** Eat a wide range of foods to ensure you're getting various nutrients. This includes many fruits and vegetables, whole grains, lean proteins, and healthy fats.

- **Mind Your Macros:** Balance your intake of macronutrients (carbohydrates, proteins, and fats) according to your body's needs. Carbohydrates are essential for energy, proteins for repair and growth, and fats for brain health and hormone production.

2. FOCUS ON GUT HEALTH:

- **Fiber-Rich Foods:** Include plenty of fiber from vegetables, fruits, legumes, and whole grains. Fiber supports digestive health and feeds beneficial gut bacteria.

- **Probiotics and Prebiotics:** Incorporate fermented foods like yogurt, kefir, sauerkraut, and kimchi for probiotics and foods like bananas, onions, and garlic for prebiotics.

3. MINDFUL EATING:

- **Listen to Your Body:** Pay attention to hunger and fullness cues. Eating mindfully helps prevent overeating and enhances the enjoyment of meals.

- **Reduce Processed Foods:** Limit intake of highly processed foods, which often contain high levels of sugar, unhealthy fats, and additives that can negatively impact physical and mental health.

4. HYDRATION:

- **Stay Hydrated:** Adequate water intake is crucial for physical health and cognitive function. Aim for at least 8 glasses of water daily, more if you're active or live in a hot climate.

5. KEY NUTRIENTS FOR MENTAL HEALTH:

- **Omega-3 Fatty Acids:** Found in fish, flaxseed, and walnuts, these are vital for brain health and may help reduce the risk of depression.

- **B Vitamins:** Important for energy production and brain health. Include sources like whole grains, meat, eggs, and leafy greens.

- **Magnesium and Zinc:** Essential for mood regulation and found in nuts, seeds, legumes, and whole grains.

6. REGULAR MEALS:

- **Consistency in Eating:** Eating at regular intervals helps maintain blood sugar levels, which is important for mood stability and energy.

7. LIMIT STIMULANTS:

- **Moderate Caffeine and Sugar:** Excessive consumption can lead to energy crashes and mood swings.

8. SUPPLEMENTATION:

- **Consider Supplements:** Supplements might be helpful if your diet lacks certain nutrients. However, consulting with a healthcare provider before starting any supplements is best.

Nutrition is never a one-size-fits-all practice. It's all about finding what works best for your body and lifestyle. Additionally, while nutrition is key to overall well-being, it's most effective when combined with other healthy lifestyle practices like regular physical activity, adequate sleep, and stress management techniques.

WILL NUTRITION HELP THE SOMATIC THERAPY OUTCOME?

Yes, integrating a thoughtful nutrition plan alongside somatic therapy can significantly help in managing stress and trauma. When undergoing somatic therapy, your body is learning to release and process deep-seated tensions and traumas. Proper nutrition supports this process by ensuring your body and brain have the resources to heal and rebuild. For instance, omega-3 fatty acids and B vitamins play crucial roles in brain health and can support mood regulation and cognitive function, aiding in managing stress and trauma. Magnesium, often referred to as the 'relaxation mineral', helps in muscle relaxation and stress reduction, which can be particularly beneficial when dealing with physical manifestations of trauma.

Furthermore, a diet rich in antioxidants from fruits and vegetables can combat oxidative stress, which is often elevated in individuals with chronic stress and trauma. Regular, balanced meals help stabilize blood sugar levels, preventing mood swings and irritability often associated with hunger and erratic eating patterns. Hydration is equally critical; even mild dehydration can increase cortisol levels, the body's primary stress hormone.

Moreover, mindful eating—paying close attention to the taste, texture, and sensations of your food—can be a form of mindfulness practice, helping to ground and calm the mind, which is beneficial for those dealing with trauma. It's important to remember that while nutrition is a powerful tool, its greatest benefits are seen when it's part of a comprehensive approach, including somatic therapy and other supportive practices. As you continue your somatic therapy, a well-considered nutrition plan will provide the physical substrates for healing and reinforce the psychological and emotional work you're undertaking, leading to a more resilient and balanced state of being.

Yoga and Somatic Integration: Aligning Mind, Body, and Spirit

Yoga, an ancient practice originating over 5,000 years ago in India, has evolved significantly to become a holistic approach that aligns closely with the principles of somatic therapy. Initially centered on spiritual and mental development, yoga's physical aspect, known as Hatha Yoga, gained prominence and is now widely recognized for its benefits in harmonizing the body and mind. This mind-body connection is a cornerstone of yoga and somatic therapy, focusing on resolving physical tensions and traumas through heightened bodily awareness.

Intriguingly, regular yoga practice has been shown to influence brain plasticity, leading to structural changes in the brain, particularly in areas related to pain processing, body awareness, and stress regulation. This aligns perfectly with somatic therapy's objective of rewiring the brain's response to trauma and stress. Some yoga practices are specifically tailored for trauma recovery, like Trauma-Sensitive Yoga (TSY), which aids in regaining bodily comfort, reducing PTSD symptoms, and improving mental health.

A crucial element of yoga, pranayama or breath control, is pivotal in activating the parasympathetic nervous system, thus fostering relaxation and stress reduction – key aspects in dealing with trauma. Furthermore, yoga enhances interoception, the awareness of internal bodily sensations, a skill vital in somatic therapy for becoming more attuned to physical sensations and emotional states, essential in processing and healing from trauma.

Yoga's adaptability to various needs and abilities makes it a versatile tool in therapeutic settings, offering different styles, from gentle, restorative yoga to more dynamic forms. This adaptability, combined with its focus on fostering a deeper connection with oneself, makes yoga an invaluable complement to somatic therapy, providing a comprehensive approach to healing that addresses both the physical and mental facets of trauma and stress.

YOGA AND TRAUMA

Yoga's role in trauma healing is profound and multifaceted, particularly in how it helps release trauma stored in the body. Traumatic experiences often leave physical imprints, manifesting as chronic tension, disrupted breathing patterns, and a heightened or numbed stress response. Yoga offers a pathway to address and release these physical manifestations of trauma through its integrated practices of physical postures (asanas), breath control (pranayama), and meditation.

The asanas in yoga encourage mindfulness and body awareness, allowing individuals to gently explore and release bodily tensions. This physical engagement helps in reconnecting with the body, which is often a significant challenge for those who have experienced trauma and may feel detached or dissociated from their physical selves. Pranayama, or controlled breathing, is particularly effective in regulating the nervous system. It helps shift the body from a state of heightened arousal, common in trauma survivors, to a more relaxed and grounded state. This regulation is crucial in trauma recovery, as it aids in re-establishing a sense of safety and control.

Moreover, yoga's meditative aspects foster a calm, present-focused mindset, which can be therapeutic for individuals dealing with trauma-related anxiety and intrusive thoughts. The practice encourages a non-judgmental awareness of the present moment, helping individuals to process and gradually heal from their traumatic experiences.

Integrating yoga into trauma therapy, therefore, not only addresses the psychological aspects of trauma but also actively involves the body in the healing process, acknowledging and utilizing the deep connection between physical and mental well-being in overcoming the effects of trauma.

YOGA AND SOMATIC INTEGRATION

Somatic integration is a therapeutic approach that focuses on integrating the mind, body, and spirit to promote overall health and well-being. Yoga can facilitate somatic integration by bridging the mind, body, and spirit, thus promoting holistic healing. At its core, yoga is a practice deeply rooted in the philosophy of mind-body unity.

In yoga, asanas serve as a tool for developing bodily awareness. Practitioners learn to notice and interpret physical sensations, understand their bodies' capabilities and limitations, and release physical tension. This heightened awareness fosters a deeper connection with the body, allowing for the recognition and potentially the release of stored emotions or trauma, a key aspect of somatic therapy.

Breathwork in yoga, or pranayama, is another crucial element in facilitating somatic integration. Controlled breathing exercises help regulate the nervous system, shifting from the sympathetic 'fight or flight' response to the parasympathetic "rest and digest" state. This regulation is essential in managing stress, anxiety, and emotional imbalances, offering a pathway to mental and emotional healing through physical means.

Additionally, meditative yoga practices encourage mindfulness and present-moment awareness, which are integral to understanding and processing emotional and psychological experiences. This mindfulness helps break down barriers between mental and physical states, fostering an integrated, holistic approach to well-being.

By harmoniously blending these elements, yoga becomes a powerful medium for somatic integration, allowing individuals to explore and unite their physical, mental, and emotional aspects in a supportive, healing environment.

WHERE TO START

A good starting point for beginners interested in using yoga for somatic integration involves a gradual, mindful approach that prioritizes bodily awareness and comfort. Here are some key steps to begin this journey:

1. **Start with Gentle Yoga Styles:** Explore gentle forms of yoga such as Hatha, Yin, or Restorative Yoga. These styles focus on slow

movements, deep stretching, and mindful breathing, making them ideal for beginners and fostering body awareness.

2. **Focus on Breathwork:** Learn the basics of pranayama (breath control). Breathing exercises are a core part of yoga and crucial for somatic integration. They help regulate the nervous system, reduce stress, and enhance body-mind connection.

3. **Incorporate Mindfulness:** Practice mindfulness both on and off the yoga mat. During each pose, pay attention to your bodily sensations, thoughts, and emotions. This awareness is key to somatic integration, as it helps you connect with your inner self.

4. **Join Beginner-Friendly Classes:** Consider joining a beginner's yoga class or workshop. A knowledgeable instructor can guide you through the basics, ensure you're performing poses correctly, and provide modifications to suit your level of comfort and ability.

5. **Create a Comfortable Practice Space:** Set up a quiet, comfortable space for your practice. A calm environment helps in maintaining focus and deepening your practice.

6. **Listen to Your Body:** Be attentive to your body's signals and limitations. Avoid pushing yourself into discomfort or pain. Yoga is about harmony and balance, not competition or strain.

7. **Consistency is Key:** Regular practice, even if it's just a few minutes a day, can be more beneficial than longer, infrequent sessions. Consistency helps in gradually building strength, flexibility, and mindfulness.

8. **Explore Online Resources:** Utilize online resources such as videos for beginners, yoga apps, or virtual classes, especially if attending in-person classes is not feasible.

9. **Integrate Yoga with Daily Life:** Try to incorporate the principles of yoga into your daily life. Mindfulness, deep breathing, and stretching can be practiced throughout the day to maintain the mind-body connection.

10. **Be Patient and Open-Minded:** Remember that yoga and somatic integration progress is a personal journey. It takes time and

patience. Be open to the experiences and changes that come with the practice.

Starting with these steps, yoga can be a valuable tool for somatic integration, aiding in developing a deeper understanding of the body-mind connection and promoting overall well-being.

Expressive Arts Therapy: Tapping into Creative Healing

Expressive arts refer to a therapeutic approach that uses various forms of creative expression to foster emotional healing and personal growth. This method is grounded in the idea that creative expression can be a powerful means to explore and understand emotions, develop self-awareness, and improve mental health. The expressive arts typically encompass a range of creative disciplines, including:

1. **Visual Arts:** This includes painting, drawing, sculpture, and collage. Engaging in visual arts allows individuals to express thoughts and feelings nonverbally, often revealing insights that might not emerge through traditional talking therapies.

2. **Music:** Engaging with melodic tunes can be therapeutic. It can help in expressing emotions, reducing stress, and improving mood.

3. **Dance and Movement:** Dance and movement therapy involves using body movements as a form of expression. This can be particularly helpful in releasing bodily tension, improving physical awareness, and exploring emotions often held in the body.

4. **Drama:** This includes role-playing, improvisation, and storytelling. Drama therapy can help individuals explore their life situations, express feelings, and gain insight into their behavior and the behavior of others.

5. **Writing and Poetry:** Expressive writing, including journaling or poetry, offers a way to articulate thoughts and feelings. It can be a powerful tool for processing emotions and experiences.

6. Photography and Digital Media: Using photography or digital media as a creative expression allows individuals to capture and reflect on their perceptions of the world and themselves.

Expressive arts therapy is often used in combination with other therapeutic approaches and can be particularly effective in treating emotional trauma, anxiety, depression, and other mental health issues. It offers a holistic approach to healing, recognizing that creativity can be a gateway to understanding and healing the deeper layers of the psyche. This therapy is inclusive and adaptable, making it suitable for people of all ages and abilities.

THE CONCEPT OF CREATIVE HEALING

Creative healing is a therapeutic concept that revolves around creative processes to foster emotional, mental, and sometimes physical healing. This approach is grounded in the belief that creative expression can be a powerful tool for personal growth and recovery. It encompasses various forms of artistic expression, such as painting, writing, music, dance, drama, and other creative arts.

The core idea of creative healing is that engaging in creative activities provides an alternative outlet for expressing feelings and experiences that might be difficult to articulate through conventional language. This form of expression can be particularly liberating for individuals dealing with trauma, emotional blockages, or psychological disorders. By creating art, individuals can externalize their internal experiences, gaining new insights and perspectives on their emotions and thought patterns.

Creative healing also fosters a sense of mindfulness and presence as individuals focus on it. This focus can be therapeutic in itself, offering a respite from stress and anxiety. It encourages a non-judgmental approach to one's experiences and emotions, promoting self-acceptance and self-compassion.

Moreover, the creation process in creative healing is often more important than the end product. It is the act of exploring, experimenting, and expressing that brings therapeutic value rather than the pursuit of an aesthetically pleasing outcome. This aspect of creative healing makes it accessible and beneficial to everyone, regardless of artistic skill or experience.

Creative healing is not limited to formal therapy settings; it can be incorporated into daily life as a self-care practice. Whether journaling, engaging in a hobby, or simply doodling, these creative activities can contribute to an individual's overall well-being by providing a healthy channel for coping with life's challenges. This approach aligns well with holistic and integrative health philosophies, which recognize the interconnectedness of the mind, body, and spirit in achieving overall health and happiness.

HOW EXPRESSIVE ARTS COMPLEMENT SOMATIC THERAPY

Expressive arts can significantly complement and enhance somatic therapy by providing alternative avenues for expression and healing, particularly for emotions and experiences that are difficult to articulate in words. Here's how expressive arts can be integrated with somatic therapy:

1. **Non-Verbal Expression:** Somatic therapy focuses on the physical manifestations of emotional and psychological experiences. Expressive arts add another layer to this by offering non-verbal modes of expression. Activities like drawing, painting, or dance allow individuals to externalize and process emotions that are 'stored' in the body but may not be easily verbalized.

2. **Body Awareness and Movement:** Dance and movement therapies, integral parts of expressive arts, directly align with the somatic approach by focusing on bodily sensations and movements. These practices can help release physical tension, enhance body awareness, and explore the connection between physical sensations and emotional states.

3. **Accessing Subconscious Material:** Creative activities can tap into the subconscious mind, bringing to the surface underlying issues and emotions. This is particularly beneficial in somatic therapy,

where the focus is often on uncovering and healing deep-seated emotional wounds.

4. **Emotional Release and Catharsis:** Engaging in expressive arts can be cathartic. For instance, dramatizing personal experiences or using music for emotional expression can provide a safe outlet for releasing pent-up emotions, contributing to the healing process in somatic therapy.

5. **Mindfulness and Presence:** Many forms of expressive arts require mindfulness and present-moment awareness, which are key components in somatic therapy. Practices like mindful drawing or focused musical composition can enhance one's ability to stay grounded and present, a crucial skill in processing trauma and stress.

6. **Improving Self-Reflection and Insight:** Creating art can lead to increased self-awareness and insight. Reflecting on one's artwork or creative output can provide new perspectives on personal challenges and experiences, aiding in the therapeutic process.

7. **Enhancing Coping Skills:** Expressive arts offer tools and skills that individuals can use outside therapy sessions. For example, journaling, simple drawing exercises, or mindful photography can be used as coping mechanisms to manage stress and emotional upheavals in daily life.

Therapists can provide a more holistic treatment approach by incorporating expressive arts into somatic therapy. This combination allows for a broader exploration of an individual's experiences and emotions, addressing both the physical and psychological aspects of healing.

Chapter Summary

In concluding this chapter, we have journeyed through the interconnected realms of nutrition, yoga, and creative healing, exploring their collective impact on somatic therapy and holistic well-being. Initially, we delved into nutrition, understanding its pivotal role in physical and mental health. A balanced diet, rich in essential nutrients, nourishes the body and supports emotional stability and mental clarity. This nutritional foundation sets the stage for effective somatic therapy, providing the energy and biochemical balance needed for healing and resilience.

Next, we focused on yoga, a practice that embodies the essence of the mind-body connection. Yoga, with its blend of physical postures, breathwork, and meditation, is a powerful tool in somatic therapy. It aids in releasing physical tensions associated with emotional traumas and facilitates a deeper awareness of bodily sensations and emotional states. Yoga's ability to regulate the nervous system and enhance mindfulness makes it an invaluable component of healing, aligning physical health with mental and emotional well-being.

Finally, we explored the realm of creative healing – a therapeutic approach that harnesses the power of artistic expression. Through mediums like painting, music, dance, and writing, creative healing allows for expressing emotions and experiences that might be difficult to articulate verbally. This therapy is particularly effective in accessing and processing subconscious material, offering a cathartic release and a path to deeper self-understanding. When integrated with somatic therapy, creative healing provides a holistic approach to treatment, addressing not just the symptoms but the root causes of emotional and psychological distress.

Together, nutrition, yoga, and creative healing form a triad of complementary practices that enrich the journey of somatic therapy. They underscore the importance of addressing all aspects of an individual – physical, mental, and emotional – in the pursuit of health and healing. This holistic approach is central to somatic therapy, promoting a balanced and harmonious state where true healing and personal growth can flourish.

Chapter 12

Long-Term Strategies for Sustained Healing

As we turn the page to the next chapter of our exploration into the healing journey, we focus on the long-term strategies that foster sustained healing and growth. While the initial phases of therapy are often about addressing acute issues and finding stability, this chapter is dedicated to the ongoing journey – the cultivation of resilience, the prevention of relapse, and the continuous pursuit of personal development beyond the therapy sessions.

We'll review the core of what it means to not just survive but thrive in the face of life's challenges. Resilience isn't a trait that individuals have or don't have; it involves behaviors, thoughts, and actions that can be learned and developed. This section will explore strategies to fortify emotional resilience, turning the lessons from somatic therapy into enduring strengths.

Moving on, we recognize that healing isn't a linear journey, and relapses are bound to happen. Setbacks are a natural part of life, but they don't have to derail the progress made in therapy. This section will provide practical advice to maintain the gains from therapy and effectively navigate the challenges that might arise.

Lastly, we'll discuss how the end of formal therapy doesn't mean the end of personal growth. Healing is a lifelong journey with continuous opportunities for learning and self-discovery. This section will inspire you to embrace a mindset of ongoing growth, exploring how the principles learned in therapy can be applied to all areas of life, leading to a more fulfilling and purposeful existence.

Together, these sections will equip you with a deeper understanding and a comprehensive toolkit for sustained healing and growth, ensuring that self-discovery and improvement continues well beyond the therapy room.

Building Resilience: Strengthening Emotional Foundations

Resilience is a dynamic and crucial trait characterized by the ability to bounce back from adversity, trauma, or significant stress. It's about adaptability, emotional awareness, and an optimistic outlook combined with effective problem-solving skills. Resilient individuals are adept at regulating their emotions and possess a proactive approach to challenges, constantly finding ways to adapt and persevere. A hallmark of resilience is the presence of strong, supportive social networks. Having people to rely on for emotional and practical support significantly bolsters an individual's resilience.

Central to resilience is the concept of self-efficacy – the belief in one's ability to handle and overcome challenging situations. This confidence is intertwined with a flexible mindset, allowing resilient people to maintain perspective and adjust their strategies as needed. They learn from past experiences and remain open to new ideas and approaches.

Self-care also plays a pivotal role in fostering resilience. It encompasses not just physical care like adequate sleep and exercise but also mental and emotional self-care practices such as mindfulness or engaging in enjoyable activities. Furthermore, resilient individuals often find strength in a sense of meaning or purpose, especially during difficult times. This sense of purpose can transform challenges into opportunities for personal growth and contribution.

Moreover, resilience involves a degree of acceptance, recognizing that not all situations are within one's control and that adversity is a part of life. Building resilience is not a static achievement but a continuous personal development process. It involves nurturing various aspects of one's life and psyche, enhancing the ability to navigate life's complexities with greater ease and confidence.

UNDERSTANDING EMOTIONAL FOUNDATIONS

People's emotional foundations are based on a combination of factors that shape how they experience, express, and manage their emotions. These foundations are often established early in life and are influenced by various elements:

1. **Early Childhood Experiences:** A person's experiences and relationships in early childhood play a crucial role in shaping their emotional foundations. Secure attachment with caregivers, consistent emotional support, and positive social interactions contribute to a strong emotional foundation.

2. **Family Dynamics and Environment:** A family's emotional tone and dynamics influence a person's emotional development. Growing up in a family where emotions are openly discussed and validated helps build healthy emotional skills. Conversely, environments where emotions are ignored or punished can lead to challenges in emotional regulation.

3. **Cultural and Societal Norms:** Cultural background and societal

norms significantly impact how emotions are perceived and expressed. Different cultures have varied expectations and norms regarding emotional expression, which can shape an individual's emotional experiences and expressions.

4. **Education and Learning:** Formal and informal education, including learning from parents, teachers, and peers, contributes to the development of emotional intelligence. Skills like empathy, emotional regulation, and communication are often learned through social interactions and educational settings.

5. **Life Experiences and Traumas:** Personal experiences, including traumas, significantly influence emotional foundations. Traumatic events can disrupt emotional development, leading to challenges like heightened anxiety or difficulty in trusting others. Conversely, overcoming challenges can strengthen emotional resilience.

6. **Biological and Genetic Factors:** Genetics and biology also play a role. For instance, some aspects of temperament are innate and can predispose individuals to certain emotional responses.

7. **Self-Perception and Self-Esteem:** How individuals perceive themselves and their self-esteem affects their emotional foundation. A positive self-image and high self-esteem generally lead to healthier emotional coping strategies.

8. **Mental Health:** Overall, mental health is a crucial factor. Conditions like depression or anxiety can affect how emotions are processed and regulated.

9. **Support Systems:** The presence or absence of supportive relationships in life, including friends, family, and community, shapes emotional coping mechanisms and resilience.

10. **Personal Beliefs and Values:** An individual's beliefs and values, often influenced by their upbringing and experiences, play a role in how they interpret and react to emotional experiences.

These factors combine uniquely for each individual, creating a complex and dynamic emotional foundation, and can be key in personal growth and developing healthier emotional responses and relationships.

CULTIVATING RESILIENCE

Strengthening emotional foundations and cultivating resilience is vital to personal development and well-being. This process involves both understanding and nurturing various aspects of oneself. Here's a guide to help you through this process:

1. **Develop Self-Awareness:** The first step is to understand your emotions, triggers, and responses. This can be achieved through practices like mindfulness and reflection. Keeping a journal can be a helpful tool for self-discovery and understanding patterns in your emotional responses.

2. **Practice Emotional Regulation:** Learn techniques to manage intense emotions. This can include deep breathing, meditation, or progressive muscle relaxation. Over time, these practices can help reduce the intensity of emotional reactions and increase the ability to handle stress more effectively.

3. **Build a Supportive Network:** Cultivate relationships with friends, family, or community groups that provide emotional support. Sharing your experiences with people who offer understanding and encouragement is crucial for emotional resilience. In strengthening emotional foundations, focusing on nurturing positive relationships and minimizing exposure to toxic or unhealthy relationships is essential. This might involve setting boundaries or seeking new relationships that are more supportive and nurturing.

4. **Develop Positive Thinking:** Cultivating a positive outlook can significantly impact resilience. This doesn't mean ignoring the negatives but rather focusing on solutions and learning from setbacks. Techniques like cognitive restructuring can be beneficial, where negative thoughts are challenged and replaced with more positive, realistic ones.

5. **Embrace Challenges as Opportunities:** View challenges as opportunities for growth. This shift in perspective can transform the way you approach obstacles, turning them into learning experiences rather than insurmountable problems.

6. **Prioritize Self-Care:** Regular self-care practices are essential. This includes adequate sleep, nutrition, exercise, and engaging in hobbies or activities that bring joy. Self-care is not selfish; it's necessary to maintain physical and mental health.

7. **Seek Professional Help When Needed:** Sometimes, the guidance of a therapist or counselor can be invaluable in working through emotional challenges and building resilience. They can provide tools and strategies tailored to your needs and help you navigate difficult times.

8. **Continuous Learning and Growth:** Adopt a mindset of lifelong learning. Attend workshops, read books, or engage in conversations that challenge and inspire you. This commitment to personal development contributes significantly to emotional resilience.

By integrating these practices into your daily life, you gradually build a stronger emotional foundation. It requires continuous effort and self-compassion. Each step forward in this journey enhances your capacity to cope with current challenges and prepares you for future ones, leading to a more fulfilling and resilient life.

Preventing Relapse: Strategies for Maintaining Progress

Relapses are a natural and common aspect of the healing process, particularly in the context of emotional, psychological, or behavioral challenges. Healing is rarely a linear journey; it often involves a series of ups and downs, progress, and setbacks. This understanding is crucial in managing expectations and developing long-term recovery strategies.

A relapse can be defined as a return to previous patterns of behavior or a decrease in functioning after a period of improvement. In the context of mental health or emotional healing, this might mean experiencing symptoms again after a period of feeling better. For instance, someone recovering from depression might have periods of returning symptoms, or someone working through anxiety might experience a resurgence of anxiety attacks.

Recognizing that a relapse doesn't signify failure or a reversal of all progress is important. Rather, it can be viewed as part of the natural healing cycle and a learning opportunity. Each relapse can provide valuable insights into triggers, vulnerabilities, and the effectiveness of coping strategies. This understanding can guide further refinement and adjustment of treatment plans or coping strategies.

Furthermore, acknowledging the possibility of relapse can be empowering. It prepares individuals to face setbacks with a more resilient mindset and equips them with strategies to navigate them. Building a support system, continuing therapy or counseling, and maintaining self-care routines are critical in managing and minimizing the impact of relapses.

Ultimately, the goal is not to achieve a state of permanent, unchanging wellness, as this is unrealistic for most people. Instead, the aim is to develop resilience and skills to effectively manage and bounce back from setbacks. Over time, as these skills are strengthened and as individuals gain deeper insights into their healing process, the frequency and intensity of relapses often decrease, leading to more sustained periods of well-being.

RELAPSE PREVENTION STRATEGIES

Preventing relapses, in the long run, involves a combination of strategies that focus on maintaining progress and building resilience. Here are some effective strategies:

1. **Ongoing Self-Care:** Regular self-care is crucial. This includes maintaining a healthy lifestyle with balanced nutrition, regular exercise, adequate sleep, and engaging in joy and relaxation activities. Self-care acts as a buffer against stress and helps maintain emotional balance.

2. **Mindfulness and Awareness:** Developing mindfulness helps

recognize early signs of a potential relapse. Awareness of your thoughts, feelings, and bodily sensations enables you to identify and address issues before they escalate.

3. **Stress Management:** Since stress can be a significant trigger for relapse, learning and regularly practicing stress management techniques such as deep breathing, meditation, or yoga can be extremely beneficial.

4. **Support Systems:** Maintain and nurture a strong support system. Stay connected with friends, family, or support groups who understand your journey and can offer encouragement and perspective during challenging times.

5. **Ongoing Therapy or Counseling:** Continuing with therapy or counseling sessions, even after significant progress, can provide continuous support and guidance. It also offers a safe space to discuss potential triggers or challenges and develop coping strategies.

6. **Educate Yourself:** Understanding your condition, triggers, and symptoms can empower you to take charge of your health. Education can come from reading, workshops, support groups, or discussions with healthcare professionals.

7. **Healthy Routines and Habits:** Establish and stick to routines that promote well-being. Consistent daily and weekly routines can provide a sense of stability and normalcy, which can be especially helpful during stress.

8. **Coping Strategies:** Develop and regularly practice coping strategies for dealing with symptoms or triggers. This might include techniques learned in therapy, such as cognitive-behavioral strategies, or personal strategies, like journaling or engaging in a hobby.

9. **Setting Realistic Goals:** Set achievable and realistic goals for yourself. This helps maintain a sense of purpose and direction, which is important for mental health and well-being.

10. **Avoiding Risky Situations:** Be mindful of situations, environments, or even people that may increase the risk of relapse and, where possible, take steps to avoid or manage them effectively.

Remember, these strategies aim not to eliminate the possibility of a relapse, as ups and downs are a natural part of life. Rather, they strengthen your ability to manage challenges and bounce back more quickly should setbacks occur.

Continuing the Journey Beyond Therapy: Lifelong Learning and Growth

After the conclusion of somatic therapy, life should ideally shift into a phase characterized by ongoing self-awareness and continuous personal growth. The insights and skills gained during therapy are not just meant for the duration of the sessions but should be woven into the fabric of daily life. This period is marked by a deeper understanding of the mind-body connection, and this awareness should continue to be nurtured through regular practices such as yoga, tai chi, or other mindful movements that encourage bodily awareness.

Emotional regulation, a key component learned in somatic therapy, should remain a consistent practice. Techniques like deep breathing, mindfulness, and meditation can become daily tools for managing stress and regulating emotional responses. Regular self-reflection helps maintain the heightened level of self-awareness achieved during therapy. Practices such as journaling or mindful meditation can be effective for ongoing introspection.

Maintaining healthy lifestyle choices is also crucial. This includes a balanced diet, regular physical activity, and adequate rest, all of which support physical and mental health. Furthermore, sustaining healthy social connections is essential. Continued engagement with supportive networks – be it friends, family, support groups, or social clubs – provides a sense of community and a framework for shared experiences and support.

Post-therapy life is also an opportunity for lifelong learning and personal development. This could involve reading, participating in workshops, or exploring new experiences that challenge and expand personal perspectives. Setting new personal and professional goals is also important in this phase. These goals should reflect the growth achieved during therapy and align with future aspirations.

As you begin to move forward from somatic therapy, remember that you will be equipped with invaluable tools and insights to navigate the complexities of life. This journey is yours to shape, filled with opportunities for growth, learning, and joy. Embrace each day with the resilience and mindfulness you've cultivated and know you have the strength to face whatever comes your way. Your path of healing and growth is a testament to your courage and commitment to a healthier, more fulfilling life. Keep moving forward, one step at a time, with confidence and hope.

My Note

Chapter 13

Community and Collective Healing

The role of community and collective healing is a vital yet often overlooked aspect of healing and personal growth. This chapter invites us to broaden our perspective, moving beyond the individual journey to consider the powerful impact of our interconnectedness. Here, we delve into the understanding that healing is a solitary endeavor and a communal experience.

The significance of community in our lives cannot be overstated – it shapes our experiences, beliefs, and behaviors. In this chapter, we'll uncover how a community's support, empathy, and shared experiences can be transformative, contributing to both individual and collective well-being. This exploration is an invitation to view healing through a wider lens, acknowledging that as we heal ourselves, we contribute to the healing of our communities, and as our communities heal, they, in turn, support us in our personal journeys.

This chapter is about recognizing the strength in togetherness and how our connections with others can foster resilience, understanding, and growth. It's a journey to discovering the symbiotic relationship between personal healing and the community's wellbeing.

Group Therapy and its Therapeutic Benefits

Group therapy is a form of psychotherapy where a small, structured group of individuals meets regularly under the guidance of a trained therapist to discuss and explore their issues and provide mutual support. It offers a unique environment for personal growth and problem-solving, differing from individual therapy in several ways:

1. **Collective Experience:** In group therapy, participants share their experiences and challenges with others facing similar issues. This collective environment fosters a sense of understanding and belonging as members realize they are not alone in their struggles.

2. **Diverse Perspectives:** Group members can offer a variety of perspectives, which can help an individual see their problems in a new light. This diversity can lead to insights and solutions that may not arise in individual therapy.

3. **Support and Encouragement:** There's a strong element of mutual support in group therapy. Members often feel encouraged and uplifted by the empathy and understanding of their peers, which can be a powerful component of the healing process.

4. **Feedback and Interaction:** The group setting allows for real-time feedback and member interaction. This dynamic can help individuals learn how to relate to others and practice new behaviors within a safe, supportive environment.

5. **Learning Through Others:** Participants can learn vicariously through the experiences and coping strategies of others in the group. Observing how others handle similar problems can provide new strategies and inspiration.

6. Cost-Effectiveness: Group therapy is often more cost-effective than individual therapy, making it a more accessible option for some people.

7. Skill Development: Many group therapy sessions focus on developing specific skills, such as social skills, stress management, or coping strategies for specific issues like anxiety or addiction.

Group therapy is used to address a wide range of issues, including mental health disorders, stress, addiction, grief, and interpersonal problems. It's important to note that while group therapy can be incredibly beneficial, it's not suitable for everyone. The effectiveness of group therapy can depend on the individual's comfort with group settings and the specific nature of their concerns.

IS GROUP THERAPY VIABLE FOR SOMATIC THERAPY?

Group therapy can be a viable and beneficial option for somatic therapy, offering unique advantages suited to the goals and preferences of the individuals involved. In somatic therapy, which emphasizes the mind-body connection, the group setting facilitates shared experiences and collective learning. Many issues addressed in somatic therapy, such as chronic pain or trauma, can benefit significantly from the supportive dynamics of a group. Participants often find comfort and a sense of belonging in sharing their experiences with others who understand and relate to their struggles, which can be crucial in reducing feelings of isolation and fostering healing.

Furthermore, group therapy allows individuals to learn from each other's insights, coping strategies, and approaches to body awareness and emotional processing. This diversity of experiences enriches the therapeutic process, offering multiple perspectives and techniques. The group setting also serves as a safe space for members to practice new communication and interpersonal skills, essential to somatic healing. Additionally, group therapy tends to be more cost-effective than individual therapy, making somatic practices more accessible to a broader range of people.

However, it's important to recognize that group somatic therapy might not suit everyone. Individual preferences, the nature of the issues being addressed, and the comfort level with group interactions play significant roles in determining the effectiveness of this approach. For those who thrive in communal settings and seek the solidarity and shared learning that comes with group therapy, it can be an enriching and supportive component of their healing journey.

Cultivating Supportive Communities: Peer Support Networks

A support group or network is a collective of individuals who come together to share experiences, provide mutual support, exchange information, and sometimes offer practical help to each other. Typically, support group members face similar challenges or life experiences, such as dealing with a specific illness, undergoing recovery, or managing life changes. The benefits of having a support group are multifaceted. Firstly, it provides a sense of community and belonging, which can be incredibly reassuring for individuals who might otherwise feel isolated in their experiences. Sharing stories and struggles with those who understand and empathize can offer emotional relief and a sense of being understood and accepted.

Furthermore, support groups are often a source of valuable information and resources. Members can learn from each other's experiences, sharing tips and advice that may be practical and relevant. This exchange of information can empower individuals to make informed decisions about their situations. In addition, witnessing the successes and coping strategies of others in similar circumstances can be inspiring and motivating, providing hope and concrete examples of positive outcomes.

Building a support network involves seeking out groups or individuals with shared experiences or concerns. This can be done through various channels such as community centers, online forums, social media groups, or healthcare providers who can recommend relevant support groups. When building a support network, finding a group where you feel comfortable, safe, and respected is essential. Participation can start small, perhaps by attending meetings or observing online discussions, and gradually increasing engagement as comfort levels grow. Additionally, being open to giving and receiving support is crucial, as the strength of a support network lies in the mutual assistance and understanding among its members. Building and maintaining a support network is an ongoing process, one that evolves as individual needs and group dynamics change, but the support and solidarity it provides can be an invaluable resource in navigating life's challenges.

The Role of Culture and Traditions in Healing

The intersection of culture, tradition, and healing extends into various dimensions of health and well-being, shaping how individuals and communities understand and address their health concerns.

1. **Cultural Interpretation of Health and Illness:** Different cultures have unique ways of interpreting the causes and meanings of health and illness. Some view illness through a spiritual lens, while others focus on the balance of physical elements or energies. These interpretations can significantly influence the types of treatments and therapies sought.

2. **Traditional Healing Practices:** Many cultures have rich traditions of healing practices, which may include herbal remedies, acupuncture, Ayurveda, shamanistic practices, or prayer. These practices often emphasize a holistic approach, considering the entire person - body, mind, and spirit.

3. **Community and Social Support:** In many cultures, the community plays a crucial role in the healing process. The support and

involvement of family and community members can provide emotional comfort, practical assistance, and a sense of belonging, which are vital for recovery and well-being.

4. **Cultural Competence in Healthcare:** Recognizing the role of culture in healing, there's a growing emphasis on cultural competence in healthcare. This approach involves healthcare providers understanding and respecting cultural differences in treatment preferences and health beliefs, which can improve patient outcomes and satisfaction.

5. **Balancing Traditional and Modern Approaches:** Integrating traditional healing practices with modern medicine can be beneficial but requires careful navigation to ensure both are used safely and effectively. This integration should respect the individual's cultural beliefs while adhering to scientific evidence and medical best practices.

6. **Mental Health and Cultural Stigma:** Cultural attitudes towards mental health can greatly affect how individuals deal with mental illness. In some cultures, there may be a stigma associated with mental health issues, which can deter people from seeking help. Creating awareness and understanding within these cultural contexts is crucial for improving mental health outcomes.

7. **Personal Empowerment and Choice:** Ultimately, individuals should feel empowered to make choices about their healing journey that resonate with their cultural identity and personal beliefs. This might involve selectively adopting practices from one's culture or exploring practices from others that align with their personal healing goals.

The role of culture and tradition in healing is complex and multifaceted, embodying both potentially beneficial and challenging aspects. Culture and tradition can significantly influence how individuals perceive and approach healing. They often provide a framework for understanding illness and health, shape healing practices, and offer a sense of identity and belonging, which can be comforting and supportive during the healing process. Traditional practices, beliefs, and rituals can offer a sense of continuity and connection to one's roots, particularly grounding and reassuring.

However, it's crucial to recognize that adherence to certain cultural or traditional practices can sometimes conflict with modern medical advice or individual preferences. Sometimes, cultural stigmas or misconceptions about certain conditions can hinder open discussion and seeking help. Therefore, the impact of culture and tradition on healing can be positive and negative, depending on the context and how they are integrated with contemporary healthcare practices.

For individuals seeking to involve culture and tradition positively in their healing journey, it's important to maintain a balance. Embracing cultural practices that bring comfort, a sense of community and align with one's values can be immensely beneficial. This might involve traditional healing practices, ceremonies, or holistic approaches that complement modern medicine. At the same time, staying open to a range of healing modalities and being willing to integrate the best of traditional and contemporary practices is key.

It's also essential to critically evaluate cultural norms and practices, discerning which aspects are helpful and which might be limiting or harmful. Engaging in open dialogue with healthcare providers about one's cultural practices can ensure that the chosen healing path respects both cultural values and medical guidance. Ultimately, integrating culture and tradition in the healing process should empower individuals, respecting their unique cultural identities while supporting their overall well-being and health.

That brings us to the end of the book.

My Note

_____

_____

_____

_____

_____

_____

_____

_____

_____

_____

_____

_____

_____

_____

_____

Conclusion: Embracing Your Healing Journey

As we reach the concluding chapter of this journey, it's important to reflect on the path of healing you've embarked upon. Embracing your healing journey is about acknowledging your strengths and vulnerabilities and recognizing the courage it takes to confront and work through personal challenges. This journey is uniquely yours, filled with individual experiences and insights that shape who you are and who you will become.

To fully embrace your healing journey, start by honoring your progress, no matter how small it may seem. Each step you've taken, every moment of self-discovery, and every challenge you've faced has contributed to your growth. Remember, healing is not a destination but a continuous process of becoming more attuned to yourself and the world around you.

Allow yourself to be open to change and growth. Healing often requires stepping out of our comfort zones and challenging long-held beliefs or patterns. Embracing this process involves exploring new perspectives and adapting as you learn more about yourself. It's about building resilience, not just to bounce back from difficulties but to spring forward into new possibilities.

Acknowledge the importance of self-compassion on this journey. Be gentle with yourself during times of struggle, and celebrate your victories, no matter how small. Self-compassion is a powerful tool in healing, as it allows you to treat yourself with the same kindness and understanding that you would offer to a good friend.

Stay connected with your support network - the people who have been there for you, offering a listening ear, a shoulder to lean on, or a word of encouragement. These relationships are invaluable, providing strength and perspective when needed.

Lastly, remember that your journey of healing is an ongoing process of self-discovery and growth. Each day brings new opportunities to learn, grow, and move closer to the person you aspire to be. Embrace these opportunities with an open heart and a curious mind. Your journey is a testament to your strength and resilience, and every step you take is a step towards a more fulfilling and meaningful life.

Celebrating Progress and Growth: Acknowledging Milestones

Acknowledging milestones and celebrating growth and progress is vital to your healing journey. It's about recognizing your efforts and the changes you've undergone, no matter how small or significant they may seem. This practice is not just a form of self-recognition but also a way to reinforce positive changes and motivate continued growth.

To start, make it a habit to reflect regularly on your journey. This could be through journaling, meditation, or quiet contemplation. Look back on where you started and appreciate how far you've come. Recognize the challenges you've faced, the obstacles you've overcome, and the new understandings you've gained. Though setbacks can be milestones, they often provide valuable lessons and opportunities for deeper self-awareness.

Set aside time to celebrate your achievements. This celebration doesn't have to be elaborate – it can be as simple as treating yourself to a favorite activity, sharing your progress with a close friend or family member, or just taking a moment to savor the feeling of accomplishment. These celebrations are markers along your journey, reminding you of your capabilities and resilience.

Share your milestones with your support network. Sometimes, others can see the growth in us that we might overlook. Their perspectives can be incredibly affirming and encouraging. Whether it's a therapist, a support group, or loved ones, sharing your progress helps solidify it in your mind and allows others to celebrate with you.

Remember, growth often happens incrementally, and it's important to acknowledge the small steps and the big leaps. These small acknowledgments can motivate you to stay focused and committed to your ongoing journey.

Most importantly, approach your milestones with a sense of gratitude. Be grateful for your strength, your courage, and the support you've received along the way. This gratitude not only enhances your sense of well-being but also connects you more deeply with the world around you.

Embracing and celebrating your growth and progress is a way of honoring your journey and yourself. It reinforces a positive mindset and helps cultivate an attitude of perseverance and hope, which are invaluable in the continuous journey of healing and self-discovery.

Embracing Self-Compassion and Self-Care: The Core of Healing

Embracing self-compassion and self-care is a crucial aspect of your healing journey, providing a foundation for emotional resilience and overall well-being. Self-compassion involves treating yourself with the same kindness, concern, and support you'd offer a good friend. It's about acknowledging your imperfections, forgiving yourself for mistakes, and understanding that struggle is a universal human experience.

To cultivate self-compassion, start by practicing mindfulness. Pay attention to your inner dialogue and notice when you're being self-critical. Instead of harsh judgment or self-criticism, respond with understanding and kindness. Remember that everyone makes mistakes and faces challenges, which don't define your worth.

Another vital aspect of self-compassion is learning to be your own advocate. Speak to yourself gently and encouragingly, especially in times of stress or failure. Celebrate your successes, no matter how small, and recognize your efforts rather than just the outcomes.

Incorporate self-care into your daily routine. Self-care is about taking the time to do activities that nurture and replenish you physically and mentally. This can include a range of activities like getting enough sleep, eating nutritious food, engaging in physical activity, pursuing hobbies, or simply taking a few moments for relaxation or meditation.

Setting boundaries is also a form of self-care. Learn to say no to demands on your time and energy that are excessive, or that compromise your well-being. Permit yourself to prioritize your needs and to take the time you need for self-care.

Remember, embracing self-compassion and self-care is not selfish; it's essential. It enables you to be more present and supportive of others because you've taken care of your well-being. By treating yourself with compassion and prioritizing self-care, you build resilience and cultivate a more positive relationship with yourself, which is fundamental for ongoing healing and growth.

Moving Forward on Your Healing Path: Embracing Lifelong Transformation

This is the beginning of an ongoing journey of lifelong transformation. Your path is uniquely yours, marked by personal growth, healing, and discovery. It's a journey not defined by a final destination but characterized by continuous learning, evolving, and becoming.

Embrace this journey with an open heart and a curious mind. Allow yourself to be amazed by your strength and resilience. Remember, every experience, every challenge, and every triumph is a step towards a deeper understanding of yourself and the world around you. This journey is about transformation, not just in moments of triumph but also in times of struggle. Each step is a part of your growth, no matter how small.

As you move forward, carry with you the lessons learned, the insights gained, and the strength you've found. Let these be your guides as you navigate the complexities of life. Know that transformation is not always easy. It requires courage, patience, and, most importantly, self-compassion. Be gentle with yourself, recognizing that growth often happens in time.

Keep in mind that you are not alone on this journey. Surround yourself with people who support and uplift you, and don't hesitate to seek out new communities and experiences that enrich your life. Your story is an ever-unfolding narrative of resilience, hope, and discovery.

So, as you turn the pages of your life, embrace each new chapter with optimism and an eagerness to grow. Your journey of lifelong transformation is a beautiful, ongoing process that shapes who you are and who you will become. Celebrate it, cherish it, and step forward confidently into a future filled with endless possibilities. The path of healing and personal evolution is yours to walk, and every step is a testament to your strength and commitment to a life of meaning and fulfillment.